# The Likable, Effective, and Productive Educator

# The Likable, Effective, and Productive Educator

## *Being the Best You Can Be as an Educator*

Brett J. Novick

ROWMAN & LITTLEFIELD
Lanham • Boulder • New York • London

Published by Rowman & Littlefield
A wholly owned subsidiary of The Rowman & Littlefield Publishing Group, Inc.
4501 Forbes Boulevard, Suite 200, Lanham, Maryland 20706
www.rowman.com

Unit A, Whitacre Mews, 26-34 Stannary Street, London SE11 4AB



British Library Cataloguing in Publication Information Available

**Library of Congress Cataloging-in-Publication Data**

Names: Novick, Brett J., author.
Title: The likable, effective, and productive educator : being the best you can be as an educator / Brett J. Novick.
Description: Lanham, Maryland : Rowman & Littlefield, 2017. | Includes bibliographical references and index.
Identifiers: LCCN 2016058702 (print) | LCCN 2017010334 (ebook) | ISBN 9781475834543 (cloth : alk. paper) | ISBN 9781475834550 (pbk. : alk. paper) | ISBN 9781475834567 (electronic)
Subjects: LCSH: Teachers—Psychology. | Teaching—Psychological aspects. | Teacher effectiveness. | Communication in education. | Teacher-student relationships.
Classification: LCC LB2840 .N68 2017 (print) | LCC LB2840 (ebook) | DDC 371.102—dc23
LC record available at https://lccn.loc.gov/2016058702

∞ ™ The paper used in this publication meets the minimum requirements of American National Standard for Information Sciences Permanence of Paper for Printed Library Materials, ANSI/NISO Z39.48-1992.

Printed in the United States of America

I would like to dedicate this book to my late father Dr. William Novick who taught me how to be a father. To my parents who taught me the importance of hard work and values. My wife, Darla, who teaches me each and every day how to be a better person, parent, and spouse. To my children, Billy and Samantha, who give me hope for a future generation with pride.

I would also like to dedicate this book to the many students, parents, and educators that I have had the honor of working with over the years who have taught me so very much. Please know it has been an honor to be allowed to play a small part in their lives. The many mentors who in both education and life inspired me in every aspect of my life. Finally, a heartfelt thank you to the publishers and staff at Rowman & Littlefield for your confidence in publishing this book and you, the reader, for taking precious time out of your life to read my book. Thank you.

# Contents

# Introduction

> The art of effective listening is essential to clear communication, and clear communication is necessary to management success.—James Cash Penney

Can you be a likable educator? It seems on the surface that this is an easy task: give everyone what they want when they want it and do it well. Everyone from administrators and parents to students and teachers will like you and you will embark on a long career happily ever after.

This is a Pollyanna view of what perhaps public education was like when the one-room schoolhouse existed and education was the central hallmark of the community. Education has changed a great deal in the many decades since, making it ever more complex, now tinged with politics as well as expectations that schools are to take on as more and more of the role of "one-stop-shop," social worker, and parent.

"Likable" now has become more challenging. It does not mean to simply schmooze all the stakeholders that touch the educator's life. It means being able to display kindness and likability while tempering a strong dose of boundaries and communication skills. Administration, teaching, and educating now mean being ever more diplomatic and a leader of the community in which you work.

It requires assertiveness to avoid being crushed under waves of the multiple, and sometimes conflicting, demands that public education throws at you.

It is these same stressors that create an additional need: the recognition of time being scarce and expectations compounding in an exponential way in schools throughout the country. Standardized testing, core curriculum standards, and an almost infinite host of other reforms in education mean that the time you have available to get things done is dramatically lessened. To avoid drowning, educators must be as efficient and productive as possible. No longer do you have the luxury of time, procrastination, or negative thinking.

The rate of novice teachers who leave the profession within five years is astronomically high. A study completed in 1989 by S. J. Rozenholtz indicated this rate was as high as 30 percent for teachers. Similarly, in a 2014 report entitled *Churn: The High Cost of Principal Turnover*, it was revealed that 25 percent of administrators leave the profession after the first year while 50 percent exit after the third academic year. This costs districts approximately $75,000 for each occurrence and costs even more in terms of human investment.[1]

Burnout and frustration among administrators, teachers, and all cross-sections of educators exist concurrently with declining quality in school climates nationwide. This does not include the hordes of administrators and other educators who retire early or even choose a less rewarding profession due to the angst of the numerous anxieties that surround modern public education.

It is the hope that this book will help to provide some tools for your proverbial tool belt to assist with tackling the stressors that pelt all educators on a daily basis. We will discuss the delicate homeostasis for likability balanced with assertiveness, efficacy, and productivity. Simultaneously tempered with harmonizing your numerous responsibilities.

Additionally, we will look into how the cultural factors of a school operate within the larger dynamic of your duties in relating with your students, fellow staff, and parents. We will address how to better understand these cultural parameters and how not recognizing them can lead you down a road of unintentional negative consequences. As our schools reflect increasing cultural diversity, so must we embrace and add to our school climate the melting pot that is our country.

As an educator, you have one of the most difficult jobs in the world. You are the one who molds the future. You are the only one who the vital job of channeling a generation from children to well-balanced adults. I aspire to provide some level of support in this book to help educators recognize the critical stake you have in our world's future.

Thank you for taking this voyage with me. I hope that you will glean some ideas to add to your toolbox that you use to sculpt our pupils. For you, my educator colleagues, you not only shape the future, but you are a reflection of it as well.

## NOTE

1. Mariah Cone, "Churn: The High Cost of Principal Turnover," Academia.edu—Share Research (accessed 29 October 2016).

*Chapter One*

# What A Well-Liked, Effective, and Productive Educator Is and Isn't

> A good leader is not necessarily the most popular person in their business, but the best ones are liked because they are respected for their vision and clarity.—Alan Sugar

This book is about being a well-liked, effective, and productive educator, which is, of course, a journey and no formal destination. We all seek to be ever more productive and effective and—for many of us—to develop a better relationship with all those who cross our paths. It is a road that requires a delicate balance of developing parental trust, patience, colleague bonds, and student confidence in both you and your abilities.

Our reputation becomes everything in our field. No matter how large a district or the community in which we work and your integrity in it, is vitally important. Your good name will travel throughout a district like seeds in the wind and plant itself district-wide. A negative status, in turn, travels even faster, like a viral wildfire burning across the dry embers of social media and on the tongues of rumor.

We are all seeking a pathway and ideas to add to our proverbial tool belts to be better at our role(s) as an educator. For most of us, being an educator is more than a job. It is a passion, a lifestyle, and a primary source from which many of our most important peer relationships spring forth. Therefore, as we seek to have students as well-rounded as possible for the frenetic century ahead, we should seek nothing less than the same attributes for ourselves in the teaching profession.

If you think back to your years in elementary school (or currently when you see a young pupil in the supermarket), you are viewed primarily as a teacher, a principal, or an educator. This paradigm is thought of before anything else. Remember when you believed your teachers ate, lived, and slept within the school? (It may still seem that way with the inordinate hours put in.) The point is, first and foremost, you are a teacher and the role is inextricable from you as a person.

Along this vein, I sought to focus this book on the three aspects that are critical to reaching this goal: being liked (while being genuine), being productive (while being a team player), and being efficient (without being critical or shorttempered with others or yourself). These objectives are only a start to the never-ending horizon ahead that comes with being a lifetime learner and teacher of others. Concurrent with this ever evolving goal is an understanding of yourself and how you can fit best into a constantly dynamic system while interacting with a host of stakeholders.

First, let's turn a sharper eye on what this book seeks to address and, maybe more importantly, what it does not. We will also delve into what may be some myths and misconceptions on the topic of being "well-liked."

## A WELL-LIKED EDUCATOR IS NOT ALWAYS LOVED BY EVERYONE

A well-liked educator strives to develop meaningful relationships with the majority of colleagues and variety of stakeholders. Note that "majority" does not mean "everyone." If you attempt to change your personal ethics and values with everyone you are in contact with, you are taking the very real risk of coming across as lacking being authentic. People sense this unpredictability and, as a result, trust is compromised.

As Fred Kofman indicated in *Conscious Business: How to Build Value through Values* in 2006, "Conscious (value-based) leadership" itself is vital because it is "the strongest determinant of an effective, healthy culture."[1] Values, you see, do not change under the winds of the daily strains and pulls of the school day.

Notice, too, the title is "well-liked," not "well-loved." Why? Issues that go on throughout a school year will create disputes in which other stakeholders do not agree and do not "love" the side you uphold. Nevertheless, your goal is to maintain a good relationship with the majority of those you relate with and simultaneously maintain respect and trust among the majority of these coworkers.

Some consider "well-liked" to be the most informed person of all the gossip that goes on in the daily soap opera that can be present in some schools. They believe that sharing the latest rumors to the eagerly awaiting hordes of faculty members is being "well-liked." This may make you somewhat popular, but it does not necessarily make you "well-liked," nor does it earn respect. It can be likened to the same fleeting popularity that is found in the middle school climate our students seek to achieve false status in.

## WHY EFFECTIVE AND PRODUCTIVE?

If you are simply "well-liked," the risk is becoming little more than a schmoozer and a gossip. If you're merely "likable," your only function is to lead conversations around the archetypal water cooler or be the talk show host for the faculty room. Conversations are surface and superficial, as are the connections that are made. Similarly, these contacts are fragile and hollow.

As the sign states, "Shallow: No Diving"—a shallow person may as well have the same sign around their neck. Superficiality, as you know, is not the preferred role of the educator. Such an educator may be liked by many (at least on the surface) but respected by very few. Further, if you are not effective and don't produce the product contained within your school's climate, you are a charismatic person but a rather useless educator.

"Productive" and "effective" mean that you can balance the traits of a true teacher/leader. It is about being able to produce a product and do so effectively. Our product? Well-rounded, educated scholars, sculpted by balanced educators to foster a better generation ahead than our own.

## WHY EDUCATOR AND NOT TEACHER, ADMINISTRATOR, PARAPROFESSIONAL, THERAPIST, AND SO ON?

It takes a school system to properly educate a well-adjusted and prepared pupil for the frenetic pace and expectations of the world that lies ahead of them. The skills addressed in this book parallel very closely those needed by all educators.

If you have a reputation as being aloof or lacking relational abilities, you may fail to make connections. Concurrently, if you are unproductive or ineffective, you may fail no matter the role you play in the system of education. In short, the traits in this book are globally necessary for us all. Regardless of function within the school setting, without these attributes, you may keep treading water for a while, but you will not swim to any shore.

## SO THIS MEANS YOU WILL BE LIKED BY EVERYONE?

No, sorry, you will never reach the goal of being liked by everyone. If you look at all the numerous personalities and agendas of the people at work, you will quickly realize the diverse needs, idiosyncrasies, and personalities of all that you brush up against. Some are more assertive, and some more passive. Some are older, and some are younger. Some are there to work their way up the ladder and others are there to bide their time. Goals and objectives can seem as different as the cacophony of roles and personalities of those you work with.

Rather, the goal in this book is to provide you with the traits necessary to develop trust and bonds with the majority of those you come in contact. This objective, of simply forming the lion's share of positive bonds, suffices in most cases. As you may tell your students, "you don't have to like everyone, but you have to get along with everyone." This book will help increase the likelihood that you have the skills necessary to get along with many of those in the workplace. Some of those you happen upon will simply have irreconcilable differences that cannot be remedied completely (however, this book will improve greatly your chances of making these relationships manageable).

## DOESN'T "BEING LIKED" MEAN DIFFERENT THINGS TO DIFFERENT PEOPLE?

Yes, various cultures, environments, and school climates have different expectations of what positive relationships norms are. Therefore, we will give a brief overview of some of the multitude of the cultures and societies as well as a definition of what "liked" means.

Many times, we have our understanding of what people need to do (and not do) to get along with others. We have a leaning toward what we believe to be "right," a psychological trait known as the attribution bias (more on this later). We will learn that relationships with the diversity of people we come in contact with have equally diverse expectations of what it means to "be liked."

## WHAT IF YOU *DO* WANT EVERYONE TO LIKE YOU?

Here is the issue: having everyone like you is impossible. If you are an umbrella salesman, you hope for rain, despite everyone else wanting the sunniest of days. Each of us has our favorite coworkers, students, and parents (despite some of us denying this fact of human nature). One cannot change another's preferences and opinion(s) of you totally. However, you can greatly increase your chances of winning others over toward liking and, more vitally, respecting you. This objective will be a major portion of common intersections and the focus of this book.

## WHAT ABOUT GETTING OTHERS TO RESPECT YOU?

Now, we come to the subject of "respect" versus "likability." This book would certainly be doing you a grave disservice to imply just being liked by others is simply enough. If it did, that would stand in the way of productivity, effectiveness, and integrity as well as self-respect. If you only just want to be liked, then you would have no moral anchor and would be at the mercy of the currents of whatever tide it takes to simply "be liked" by all the contrasting expectations that pull you to and fro.

In this scenario, you lose something though. Namely, you lose self-respect and integrity. Peers, parents, and students all begin to realize you are a "pushover" and/or "yes man/woman." This not only negatively affects your ability as an educator; it also damages your reputation and ability to be trusted. Worse yet, you come down on yourself as time and time again you are not clear and honest in communications with others. One finds themselves saying, "I wish I said that. . . . I wish I didn't do that. . . . Why did I say yes to that???" You then begin to question your honesty and courage in all your dealings with others. Think of grading or teacher evaluation; if you are dishonest, you may make someone else happy, temporarily, but you have let yourself down permanently by not being frank with yourself.

## SO MUCH TO DO AND SO LITTLE TIME

Educators are under a barrage of responsibilities. It can seem like a treadmill: more and more to do, less and less time to do it. More and more is expected from the educator with dwindling time and compensation to address what are ever-growing responsibilities. If you do not have the opportunity to effectively manage your time, your time manages you. If your time manages you, it spills over into every aspect and realm of your school and personal life, and you drown in the overwhelming flood of anxiety. Your job is no longer fun or a passion; it becomes a source of dread and despair.

## WHAT IF YOU TEND TO HAVE AN AGGRESSIVE PERSONALITY AND OTHERS *DO* RESPECT YOU?

This book is partially about productive communication skills. If others are in fear of you or find you to be too aggressive to interact with, chances are they will shy away from you. Worse yet, peers will "talk around" you and you will miss vital information that your colleagues are privy. Remember, respect and intimidation are not parallel traits.

Our aim, rather, should be to lean toward the side of assertiveness in which you are capable of active listening and responding. If you are aggressive, you can't listen because you are too busy telling. With just telling, there is no learning. Without learning, you are not professing the virtue of being a lifelong learner if you already know everything there is to know.

## WHAT IF YOU TEND TO BE PASSIVE AND NO ONE RESPECTS YOU?

Our goal for this writing is to be able to be a good communicator. All of us can contribute to the realm of education. Veteran educators certainly have a lot of tools that they can share with novice teachers. Conversely, new teachers have learned "cutting-edge" modalities that they can offer to experienced teachers who are open to listening.

This being said, no one will know this unless you are able to voice your opinion clearly and assertively. If you are overly passive, you will sit at meetings or discussions and not contribute the essential information that you have to offer to your team. We will address this to help you balance your communication skills in a manner that assists you to both listen and contribute.

## DO YOU FIND YOURSELF BEING A "PRO" AT "PROCRASTINATING"?

One cannot be a "pro" at "crastinating" and be productive or effective. As more is expected of you, sometimes it just seems easier to throw up your hands, put your head in a hole, and let everything pile up on your desk.

Unfortunately, if you do this for even a short period of time, you may find yourself unable to dig out of that pile that is heaped upon you. Therefore, we will work on steps to avoid procrastinating, including ways to prioritize what you can do when you are overwhelmed.

## HOW CAN YOU AVOID GETTING OVERWHELMED?

We cannot totally inoculate ourselves from being overwhelmed at times. What one can do, however, is try to make one's self less liable to the effects of numerous expectations.

How? We will discuss how to organize and prioritize means to help juggle all of the responsibilities that are expected from you. Further, we will address how to balance that allows you to preserve the delicate equilibrium of work and family life.

## NOTE

1. Fred Kofman, *Conscious Business: How to Build Value through Values* (Boulder, CO: Sounds True, 2006).

*Chapter Two*

# The Traits of the Well-Liked Educator and How to Adopt Them

Try not be a person of success, but rather become a person of value.—Albert Einstein

## DO YOU LIKE YOURSELF?

This question may sound corny or trite, but if you do not like yourself, who you are, and the person you have become, it will be a very difficult leap to be likable. After all, if your self-esteem is low, your ability to get others to like you will also be challenging and feel false. In turn, your self-loathing rises in equal measure to your self-esteem sinking.

## BEING A GOOD LISTENER

How many times have you heard the phrase "Be a good listener"? If the many communication, self-help, and relationship books are to be believed, one must be on a seemingly endless quest to be a better listener and never reach the destination.

Fact is, good listeners are few and far between; great listeners are even rarer gems. If you want to see the plight of poor listening, go into your school's faculty room. What you will hear in these types of environment is a microcosm of difficulty with listening skills. Listen for a few moments and see:

- How many people are doing something else (e.g., reading, texting, surfing the web on their phone)?
- How many are interrupting another to tell their own even more amazing story (aka "one-upping")?
- Are conversations building off of the same topic or are they scattered with each person telling an unrelated story or statement?
- Are people making eye contact and not multitasking?
- Are people giving advice, or "trying to fix," or are they genuinely "in the moment" with those in the room?

Answering these questions honestly will tell you who is listening versus who is hearing a conversation and who is communicating versus emoting what they want to tell others.

Now, you might say that these people are simply making "small talk." While true, any level of communication to be productive it must involve talking and listening.

## The "Open-Door Policy" of Communication

Many of us have heard (or used) the expression "I have an open-door policy; my door is always open." For many, they feel that if they say they are at all times available to talk, others will see them as approachable.

Unfortunately, this is a trap that may actually prohibit good listening and communication. Initially, this may seem contrary to common sense. It may seem that the more I am available to talk, the more communication should be generated, right? People will see me as open and available.

Listening, true listening, requires a great deal of work and involves a deep amount of concentration. This means it may require preparation and to be in a proper emotional mindset to be effective. Are you always at your best mentally all the time? Unless you have found the secret for eternal peace and infinite emotional stability, the answer is probably a resounding "no."

So, when a fellow educator, parent, or student comes to see you, be certain you are prepared. This means having the time and providing the respect to offer them as much of your ability to listen as possible. Listening with half an ear or half-heartedly is perhaps worse than not listening at all. So, with that in mind, what do you say to a parent, student, or fellow educator who is asking to talk? Try these statements:

- "I would like to listen to what you are saying and want to give you 100 percent of my attention. Can I talk to you in a few minutes?" (Follow-up is vital.)
- "If this is an emergency, we can speak now. However, I want to give our conversation the time and concentration it deserves. When can we speak?"
- "This sounds like a discussion that requires some thought and time. When can we talk so we can try to figure this out together?"

You must follow up as soon as possible. You also have to be willing to give "100 percent" of you for the period of time the person in front of you is asking for and deserves.

## Be Here and Be Now

Paralleling the myth of the "open-door policy," when we are thinking of what to say next or pondering the activities of the day, we rob others of the opportunity of truly communicating directly with us. It is just as important to be able to clear your mind as it is to clear your schedule for others.

If you are thinking of the next thing you are going to do today, your grocery list, or what happened yesterday, you are not available. You are giving a student, faculty member, or parent a small percentage of you. No matter how good you are at "acting" like you are listening, you will come across as lacking genuineness.

Some of us may say, "Well, I can multitask and have become used to juggling many activities at once. I can talk to a fellow faculty member or student while shooting off an e-mail and do so while providing quality to these functions." Many of us are under the notion that multitasking is just a part of life for which many of us have a developed aptitude.

In dispelling this myth, counselor and life coach Michael J. Formica states, "The first thing to recognize is that, try as we might, we really can only do one thing at a time, so we ought to do that thing wholeheartedly.[1] Most of our time is spent in the past or the future, rather than the present moment." Therefore, focusing on more than one item (or person) at a time means trying to juggle and, ultimately, dropping the proverbial ball on the quality of all tasks and relationships.

## Don't Try to Fix What You Didn't Break

When others come to you and tell you of the problems that they are encountering, don't try to fix it . . . listen. Many times when parents or educators come to you with personal issues that are deeply painful the fix might be in the listening. Offering advice such as, "Do you know what I would do?" or, alternatively, "What you should do is . . ." minimizes the other person's problem and indicates an unwillingness on your part to listen to them.

If it can't be fixed, the fix is to just provide all your focus and empathy on listening.

## Build Trust

Do you know other educators or parents who tell you everything about everyone else? They share with you gossip, divulge personal issues they heard from peers, and negative stories. When the other faculty member is not present at lunch, they discuss them, which then brings a flurry of conversation as other teachers chime in. Conversely, a person may seek to share news about another that they are "only sharing with you" and then proceed to share it with the other hundred "you's" in the whole school.

The bottom line is if they are talking to you about others, they are also talking about you to others. This means that when you are talking to others, people are constantly assessing if you're trustworthy. If you are someone who does not speak of others when they are present and defends those who are not there to defend themselves, only then can you be deemed truly trustworthy.

## Don't Fear Silence

Many times we are fearful of silence in communication with others. We fill the air of silence with a vacuum of empty speech. When you teach an integral aspect of a lesson, put a few moments of silence at the end of it. Let that point sink in.

Paralleling this, if you are a good listener, allow time for your statements and those of others to sink in. When a teacher tells you that they have a terminal illness or a parent cries to you that their child is ill and they are overwhelmed, what is the correct response?

Be certain that you give the respect and reverence that such a comment deserves. Let it sit with you for a few minutes and be there with them in the moment. Do not try to fix, talk, or squirm out of the discomfort, just be present with them. Wait . . . listen . . . allow and revere the silence.

## Reflect Back What Is Being Said

Like the old children's game of "telephone," we hear what we want to hear, or think we heard, in a conversation. Unfortunately, we miss the minute details that someone is trying to tell us, and when we do, we miss the majority of the vital message being conveyed.

Reflecting back what is being said will show that you are listening to what is being told to you. Additionally, it will allow you to seek clarification and a firm understanding of not only what is being said, but the context of the message as well. Examples include:

- "I hear that this is really painful for you and you feel that the school is not being compassionate to your needs. Am I understanding you correctly?"
- "So what you are telling me is that your child is really struggling in Ms. Smith's class. Is that right?"
- "What you are telling me is that you are hurt that this parent criticized you on social media and you feel victimized. Am I clear on this statement?"

This manner of communication may seem artificial at first and may seem difficult to get used to. Just remember, however, the last time you attempted to call a customer service line and did not feel the representative was listening. Imagine the frustration, anger, and difficulty that you experienced when these obstacles were placed in the way of your conversation. Now you can understand the need for reflective communication in your everyday problem-solving skills.

## Reflect What Is Not Said

When you talk with someone, notice their body language. Do they have their hands crossed, their hands on their hips, legs crossed? Are they smiling, fidgeting, their head nodding?

If you subtly reflect these traits, you will gain the liking of others who see you as similar to them. A word of warning, this action must be subtle. Mirroring one's actions needs not to be confused with imitation. This means a slow and subtle transition to the respective body language you are duplicating.

Are you skeptical if this is effective or works? In an article by Vanessa Van Edwards on the Science of People website,[2] it was found that empirical study of "mirroring" led to increased tipping, more favorable initial dating, and a significantly better success rate of students who asked another to do an essay for them.

## GET TO KNOW OTHERS

Whether it be student, parent, or educator, people want to feel as though they are special and known. If you look at any well-liked or charismatic teacher, administrator, or leader, they tend to have a genuine interest in people.

This does not mean that they pretend to like other people so they can work their way up the ladder by stepping on the heads of their peers to reach the next rung. It means truly caring and recognizing others as individuals with opinions, lives, and feelings that are worthy of knowing and understanding. It also means getting to know everyone in your school system from your students, to the custodians, to those in the highest hierarchy of your school system and treating them all as equals to you and disbanding ego.

As Dale Carnegie stated so eloquently many years ago in his national best-seller, *How to Win Friends and Influence People*, "Become genuinely interested in people." The key word is "genuinely" as people can smell those who are feigning caring from a million miles away.[3]

To get to know others requires simple things like remembering names to more complicated aspects such as knowing interests, and basic aspects of what is going on in their respective lives.

It may seem too much to have these facts at hand when there are a hundred other items that you are simultaneously juggling. However, the bonds you make will be worth the time and effort that you spend. Bottom line, these issues are important because they are vital to the other parties.

## Remember Names

There is nothing more embarrassing than not knowing someone else's name. They remember yours and introduce you. In turn, you do everything to skip around the gaping issue that you are unable to recall the name of that person in front of you.

When you first meet someone, be sure to repeat their name (like we did in reflective listening). Look them in the eye and say their name again. This helps to cement a memory of the other person's name.

Also, try making a catchy rhyme or song may assist you in keeping a person's name in the grip of your mind or associating it with some catchphrase (e.g., Catchy Carol). If you do not remember someone's name, the issue becomes that the person simply is not important enough to know.

This is most clearly emphasized as we reference, again, Dale Carnegies's 1936 classic book *How to Win Friends and Influence People*, in which he writes, "A person's name is to him or her the sweetest and most important sound in any language."[4] Be certain that you are speaking their language and are fluent in doing so.

How do you remember these facts then? Write notes on your contacts on your computer or cell phone (or if you are old school on notecards) about each person that you are working with. Include facts such as:

- Names of spouse and children
- Important items of their life they have shared with you
- Concerns, celebrations, or worries that are current for them.

## A Quick Note Goes a Long Way

In the twenty-first century, we are in an e-mail and texting world. We send short, quick bursts or messages with minimal effort and recognition of the other party involved. Keep stationery on hand. When someone does something, goes out of their way, or you just want to cheer them up, leave a quick handwritten note on their desk.

You may not get a thank you; however, what you will get is a smile or someone who knows that they are not going through a difficult time alone. You may hear months or years later, "I remember that you took the time to put that note on my desk and I really needed that then. Thank you."

Paralleling this knowledge is an article written by Eric Mosely in March 2016 for the *Huffington Post* which stated, "Findings from a new survey show a direct correlation between appreciation and happiness. 86 percent of employees say they feel happier and prouder at work as a result of being recognized, while 85 percent say recognition made them feel more satisfied with their jobs."[5] Henceforth, a little note and appreciation can go a long way toward morale building.

## Smiling

The above heading is obvious, right? Most of us know that if you smile and make eye contact. This is the best way to show caring for another and getting them to like you, right? The issue is that we do not always do this.

Oftentimes, a smile is the first aspect of being open to another person. If you do not smile to your students, parents, or peers, they are not as likely to feel liked or like you in return. A smile, while simple, is often the most understated form of positive communication. It should be noted that a "canned smile," like those of the younger elementary students that are asked to smile on picture day, can be easily recognized and read by others. Practice the art of genuinely smiling, and it will carry you a long way in the realm of being liked.

## Eye Contact

Making eye contact will show you are paying attention to a peer, student, or parent. Keep in mind that constant contact can be perceived as threatening, and for some cultures, eye contact (or no eye contact at all) is considered at varying levels of appropriateness and respect (more on this later). When making eye contact, look away every few moments so as to not create the opposite effect of generating a perception of a threatening interactional dialogue.

## Touch and Personal Space

For some people, is attributed touching someone on the arm or shoulder as a form of developing an affable attitude toward another individual. Use extreme caution if you tend to be someone that is more "touchy-feely" with others.

The reason for this is because the recipient has a wide range of how they may perceive this. Does one perceive this as harassing, flirtatious, or appropriate, or does it meet with their cultural mores? All of these questions simply cannot be immediately met within the range of those with whom you come into contact. Therefore, it is best to avoid this if possible.

The same general rule applies to personal space. For some, invading of personal space (getting close to the other) increases likability and makes the other perceive warmth and closeness. For others, encroaching in their personal space is threatening and they may react aggressively.

## Making Small Talk

When meeting with a parent or peer, it is important that you are able to facilitate a degree of "small talk." Now, one might say small talk is not appropriate or that it blurs the boundaries between teacher and parent or administrator and educator. This is not the case if you keep conversations innocuous and at the surface level. It also provides a means of feeling comfortable with the other person before, perhaps, discussing issues that may be uncomfortable.

Topics that are generally safe include:

- the weather
- sports
- hobbies
- pets
- the role of school/teaching/administration

The old topics that are time-tested to lack safety in conversation include:

- politics (including those specific to your school and district)
- religion
- jokes (of even a mildly inappropriate nature)
- anything having to do with confidentiality of another person

The purpose of "small talk" is so that another can feel comfortable and willing to enter a deeper level of conversation. This may include a parent telling you about a special needs child, a teacher discussing the feeling of being overwhelmed, or an issue that is significantly affecting the family of the person you are speaking with.

## SENSE OF HUMOR

Humor has its place in getting to be well-liked in the public education forum. Remember, the teachers you had that stuck in your mind likely were the "funny ones" who knew how to employ humor. Humor, however, must be tempered. We all know a fellow faculty member (or family member) that crosses the line of funny to vulgar or humorous to corny or thinks they are being funny when in reality the laughter they receive comes at the expense of another.

That being said, humor has a definite place in being well-liked. Not taking yourself too seriously helps ease your stress as well as that of others. Humor should never be pointed at others but toward yourself. Using light-hearted humor of a self-deprecating nature helps you to ease students', parents', and fellow educators' fears.

Keep in mind that over-used humor may lead you to not be taken seriously, or others will have a figurative "rolling of the eyes" every time you walk into a room. Your objective is for comfort building and not to be the stand-up comedian of the school.

## COMPLIMENT, DON'T FLATTER

There are faculty members who lay it on thick as syrup. Flattering compliments ooze from their pores, and they are quick to tell you something about how great you are or exaggerate the positive nature of their relationship with you. There are some that fall for this empty praise, but other faculty recognize something hollow and distrusting in these comments and always questioning, "What are they going to want from me now?"

Be positive and generous in your compliments. However, be behaviorally specific about what you see in others that you like. Instead of saying generalities like, "Wow, that was a great lesson!" be specific: "I liked the way that you kept all the students engaged with that technology lesson." Don't waste an opportunity to be positive and genuine in what you say and specific in what you mean.

## DO WHAT YOU CAN WHEN YOU CAN . . . AND DON'T ANTICIPATE THAT WHAT GOES AROUND ALWAYS COMES AROUND

Many of us expect karma. "If I like everyone, everyone will like me. If I do favors for everyone, everyone will go out of their way to help me." This is especially true in the close-knit environment in the realm of public education.

What this leads to is our tacit belief that we will get an equal amount in return for those that we have helped. In believing so, we go out and try to be as nice as possible and help everyone within the school. When someone doesn't directly and reciprocally return the favor in due time, we are resentful, bitter, and angry.

We then go from an emotional high of liking everyone to a low of feeling that we are the only one who cares. We begin to suffer from "compassion fatigue," and this can quickly lead to burnout. In short, don't expect from others what you do for them. Do it because you want to; you may not get paid back with an equally emotional investment from that person and recognizing some simply don't have the emotional wealth to repay you.

Perhaps another faculty member will do something for you or give more than you gave them when you need it most. A school district is a system, a web that has many strands. Giving means not expecting in return or, conversely, getting in return when you least expect it.

## NOTES

1. Michael J. Formica, "How To Stay in the Present Moment—Don't Chop Water When You Should Be Carrying Wood," *Peace and Freedom*, 31 January 2014, https://johnib.wordpress.com/tag/dont-chop-water-when-you-should-be-carrying-wood (accessed 15 September 2016).

2. "Vanessa Van Edwards," http://www.curious.com/scienceofpeople (accessed 1 November 2016).

3. Dale Carnegie, Dorothy Carnegie, and Arthur R. Pell, *How to Win Friends and Influence People* (New York: Simon & Schuster, 1936).

4. Carnegie, Carnegie, and Pell, *How to Win Friends and Influence People.*

5. Eric Mosely, "4 Reasons Employee Appreciation Matters Year-Round," *Huffington Post*, 3 March 2016, http://www.huffingtonpost.com/eric-mosley/4-reasons-employee-apprec_b_9368584.html.

*Chapter Three*

# Developing Yourself and Your Skills as a Caring and Likable Educator

## DON'T JUDGE

The surest way to develop walls around being liked is to not like others. Judging others around you will assure this pretty quickly with a great degree of certainty. We all have preferences of one type or another that serve to distinguish us from the other faculty members in our school and district. Whether it be the type of personality you have, your opinions, or your work ethic, when these become entrenched in your mind, they become biases and we begin to judge.

Let me give you a parallel of the danger of judging: have you ever noticed that when you are driving on the highway those that drive faster than you are "crazy maniacs," while those slower are "annoying pains in the butt"? So, this means that if anyone is not going your exact speed, they are wrong? In psychology this is known as the attribution theory. That is, you tend to attribute negative or positive statements to the person themselves based on what you see as loosely defined characteristics that peeve or impress you.

Now, if we apply that to a school setting, any educator, parent, or student that does not have a similar set of beliefs as you may correspondingly be classified into a less then flattering category. When you have these beliefs deep-rooted into your own belief system, then you tend to be critical of others and look at them from a negative perspective.

With this bias in mind, you are inclined to judge and classify all those you come into contact with in your school as good or bad, right or wrong, friend or foe. In doing this, you miss that those you are looking to have a collegial relationship with or trying to teach are not just simply good or bad, right or wrong. In turn, you miss the many gray areas in conflict resolution. When you judge, you classify, and it becomes very hard to like people who are not on the same side of the fence as you. You begin to see others as issues, not parents, educators, or students. This, in turn, makes it very difficult for you to like them or be liked by them. Eventually, it leads to a downward spiral of anger and resentment towards others you work with and/or the students that you have given your life's profession to educate.

Be cautious when you begin to have the following mind-set:

"That colleague always . . ."

"That student never . . ."

"I can't stand people who . . ."

"He/she is lazy, a poor teacher/student, a (jerk, idiot, gossiper, troublemaker, fill in the blank) . . ."

## CRITICISM IS LIKE MAKING A SANDWICH

Think about the most negative statement your parent(s) ever made to you. Now, think about the most positive message they ever told you. Which is more difficult? Which is easier to recall?

Now, consider the "model" student when you went to high school, the one with a 4.0 and a perfect score on their aptitude test(s). Shift gears, and reflect on the "bad" student when you were there, the one who always got in trouble, who bullied, who did the things everyone else was afraid of doing for fear of getting in trouble.

If you are like most of us, you have an easier time recalling the negative versus the positive. For whatever reason, most of us tend to let the positive comments said to us slide off our backs while the negative stick to us like glue.

The same goes for when you need to criticize a fellow faculty member, subordinate, or pupil. If you are going to have to deliver criticism, make sure you do so "sandwiched" with as much positive in the beginning and the end of the critical comment as possible.

Now, it is not that you want to cloud your criticism with insincere rhetoric; the criticism should be direct and unclouded and offer specific steps for improvement. What is being said should also offer the same specific, direct, and unvarnished statements of positivity before and after your critical pronouncement.

## BE THANKFUL

It is easy to become jaded by the negative in the field of education. All of us know educators who become pessimistic and, in turn, sour which results in eventually being around them becomes unlikable.

Try to always feel gratitude for at least three items in school each day. The positivity you project will insulate you from the negative environment that can rain down on even the warmest of school climates. When you show thankfulness, you will tend to magnetically draw more of that trait to you as your peers and students see that you really do appreciate them and what they do. You, in turn, will be more liked because of your sincere appreciation for others.

## DON'T BE A COPY OF SOMEONE ELSE

We all have people that have mentored us. In fact, many schools and state departments of education require that a novice teacher be "mentored" by a veteran to help them learn the ropes. Our job is to "learn those ropes" and then paint our own unique signature of personality, characteristics, and strengths that make our classroom and careers of our own creation.

If you have ever copied a new document and photocopy the copies of the document over and over, you will notice something. Each duplicate of a copy that you make becomes less crisp and clear. Eventually, the copies are very poor representations of the original and become increasingly difficult to read.

In parallel, when a school climate goes south this can happen to an entire building. Some schools are popularity contests with cliques, distinct groups, leaders, and followers. Educators copy what others are doing, their thoughts, opinions, teaching styles, and even mannerisms. When this occurs, you lose those characteristics that make you the individualized educator that you are. Opinions become pushed to the wayside because everyone begins to have a mentality that they must agree and conform or be like the rest of the crowd.

If you are to be likable, do not try to "fit in" to the crowd of one party or another. If you simply adhere to the characteristics of a particular group or share their opinion just because it is popular, you may be "liked" in the short term. However, others will not trust that you are able to make your own choices or decisions and will question your sincerity, your ability to be genuine, or your willingness to remain steadfast on your established values. These, hence, are decidedly unlikable qualities in an educator. (More on this topic in a later chapter.)

## DOES BEING INTROVERTED MEAN YOU MAY BE LESS LIKABLE AS AN EDUCATOR?

No! On the contrary, there has been a significant history of leaders of every conceivable field who were deemed as leaning toward more quiet or introverted. The strength of those who have a more reserved leaning is the ability to listen more deeply and understand the system and relationships of all involved in the job.

Therefore, using this very trait (if it is an attribute of yours) will bolster your status as a leader to students, parents, and colleagues alike. An excellent read on the very power of an introverted personality is 2012's *Quiet: The Power of Introverts in a World That Can't Stop Talking*, authored by Susan Cain. In this book, the many benefits of being reserved are highlighted.[1] It details how, though emphasis is placed on the ability to be "outgoing," there is a very real need for the prowess of introverted people in all walks of life.

## BE A GOOD NEIGHBOR

This one is more common sense than anything else. Remember we have many people sharing the same building. It is akin to several tenants in any apartment complex or roommates in a large housing complex. Think back to when you shared a dorm or had roommates in your first apartment.

Don't be "that guy/gal" who leaves a mess in the faculty room, who takes food but does not contribute, that does not put something monetary in when the envelope to help a fellow faculty member rolls around a building. Or, as Jennifer Cohen of *Forbes Magazine* stated in an article so eloquently in 2014, "Keep the kitchen cleaner than you keep your own."[2]

Put even more simply: be considerate of yourself, others, and your environment. It is, and will be, noticed even if it is not voiced by those around you directly.

## BE EMPATHETIC

You never will know a student or faculty member's situation better than those directly experiencing it in the first person. Simply stating, "I understand . . ." or "What you should do (followed by unsolicited advice)" is not listening and does not increase your likability or your listening skills. Just trying to place yourself in the other's shoes and attempting to be there in that moment is the best course of action generally.

## BE A GOOD STORYTELLER

One of the best means of connecting with others is by having a few appropriate stories to tell that relate to a situation if you are trying to get a point across in a group setting.

In fact, if you look at the most eloquent and charismatic leaders of the past few centuries such as President Abraham Lincoln, Martin Luther King Jr., and, more recently, President Bill Clinton, all were great and charismatic storytellers.

"Stories and humor were nearly as important to Lincoln as oxygen and water. They were part of his life blood. Humor helped offset his natural sadness. It was literally an escape from the internal and external pressures and events of his life," wrote Donald Phillips in his book *Martin Luther King Jr. Lessons on Leadership: Inspiration and Wisdom for Challenging Times*.[3] The author makes this connection of both leaders being avid and tremendous storytellers as a means to get difficult points across without directly attacking another's views or values.

Having a few stories up your sleeve to tell about varying educational or parenting situations serves the purposes of making you more approachable as well as allowing for self-deprecating humor, which can ease a tense mood. Not to mention, when you have to do public speaking with a large group, it is a great icebreaker to the crowd.

Allowing students, parents, and faculty to know you make mistakes (contained within your stories) demonstrates your humanity and that you accept other's errors (provided they are remedied).

## AVOID COMPLAINING

We all know those at work who mull complaints over and over again in the faculty room. If the faculty room was in a basement, they would be able to make a great "whine cellar." They fail to see the positivity in their students, parents, peers, or job and, in short, suck the very joy out of a classroom, faculty room, or school in no time flat.

Before you throw your hat in the ring of volleying complaints within the faculty room, ask yourself:

- Is this statement productive to me or others?
- Does this statement add to my likability?
- Am I complaining to complain or am I trying to be part of the solution versus the problem?
- If I am complaining about a student, have I truly tried every aspect of tailoring the lesson to the student and situation?

## BE PART OF THE SOLUTION

If you are the "go to" person that others count on when they need help, you are most certainly going to be more likable. If you help others, you will get assistance in return. If you take on additional committees and commitments and assist others when they need it, you will be more liked by both those in your peer group as well as those in the hierarchy of administration at the central office.

This tendency can go awry, of course (more on this later), when you overextend yourself.

Ask yourself before you take on more than you can chew:

- Is this a part of my overall job responsibilities?
- If I give the time, is it worth the effort to my school, students, and colleagues?
- How much time will this actually take versus what I am told it will take?
- Will I be able to balance this with my current work, social, and family responsibilities?
- Am I saying “yes” to appease someone else when inside I am screaming “no”?
- Do I have to make a decision immediately, or should I wait before making a decision to see how it fits into my larger schedule?

## BE INDISPENSABLE

It goes without saying, the more indispensable you are the better. Think about it: the one who can fix the copier, knows technology, and is aware of the official (unofficial) structural hierarchy of the district becomes a vital commodity.

This is why we often say if you want to know anything, ask the school secretary. They are quite often the heart, soul, and nerve center of a school. Tapping into how to best be a school resource becomes important as you are the one who knows how to get your hands dirty and do it yourself as well.

## PEOPLE READ YOU IN MANY WAYS

We all know about body language. All of us have heard that body language and nonverbal communication accounts for a larger portion of relational interactions then actual speech. The amount varies according to psychologists and communication experts. Most agree, however, that it is the majority of how we relate with one another.

This means that when you come into a classroom, enter a hallway, or meet any of the many stakeholders that you consult with in a school day, you are already being evaluated. How you look may not be congruent to what you are thinking. Still, however, you are constantly being read (rightly or wrongly) and vice versa regardless of the incorrect or inaccurate nature as such.

When you are trying to communicate with others via body language, remember these general rules of thumb:

- Slouching/chest puffing:
    - Slouching indicates uncertainty in yourself.
    - Chest puffing indicates dominance over another individual.
- Fidgeting:
    - When you fidget with a watch, piece of clothing, phone, or any other item, it shows a lack of interest (even if it is a nervous habit).
    - Drinking, eating, texting, or other distracting activities also can be perceived as boredom.
- Crossing your arms:
    - Displays impatience or being "closed" toward discussion.
- Eye contact:
    - The right amount shows listening (though this is culturally specific).
    - No eye contact shows anger, lack of confidence, or fear of stating something.

- Excessive eye contact can be deemed aggressive.

## EGO HAS NOWHERE TO GO

All of us have some level of ego. When we say "ego," we are not talking about that far-off concept that you learned in basic psychology class in a Freudian sense. We are referring to that little voice in your head that is competitive and prideful, the voice that always has something to prove or needs to show that you are not incorrect or uneducated in any areas of life.

In schools, ego often rears its ugly head. It is no surprise that this is a frequent occurrence as public education is a complex social and political organization. People have their egos bruised as they perceive that others are out to get them, or they question the motives of those around them. We build walls, form alliances, burn bridges, and try to reestablish relational connections throughout our career.

It is so easy to get wrapped up in the "nitty-gritty" of the school climate, to be brought down by politics or raised up by the stroking of one's ego. In turn, we forget about why we are doing what we are doing and the central nature of working for the children.

## FORGIVENESS TAKES GREAT COURAGE

Forgiveness and moving on is not for the faint of heart. However, it is imperative to survive and keep a good attitude within a district. If you remember every grievance and grudge that is thrown your way, your career will be short and your memory will be long. Forgiving, but not forgetting, is the best way to assure you are able to maintain a likable persona.

If you forgive, you will be able to have a clear head as to how to proceed in your choices and your career without the clouding factor of anger and emotion. If you simply forget, though, you do not learn and you rely on being naïve of the circumstances around you, which is not a good plan either.

When egos clash (and they will), we get nowhere fast and end up infinitely butting heads without any new ideas being generated. Or, as John Baldoni stated in his 2009 *Harvard Business Review* article entitled "Managing Big Egos So the Entire Team Wins,"[4] "These are folks who are more inclined to believe in the strength of their own ideas rather than the ideas of colleagues."

## DON'T USE PAPER OR COMPUTERS TO SEND A PERSONAL MESSAGE

It is often easier to shoot off a memo or e-mail to someone than to go find them and give a message or have dialogue in person. Sometimes, we tend to hide behind a barrier of e-mails or paper memos to avoid having an uncomfortable interaction. This only leads to the idea that you are not approachable and for the stakeholders and peers to talk behind your back as well as a questioning of your bravery and integrity.

## KEEP AN OPEN MIND

When you are strongly opinionated and perceive yourself as always right, you do not have any opportunity to hear or learn other perspectives. For instance, how many times have you heard a point of view from a student or another child that seems to make perfect sense and offers a fresh perspective that you had never thought of?

Do not discount anyone's opinion as immediately wrong or force your judgments upon them. Think and listen to what they say before you offer a "knee-jerk" response or directive. The only way to grow and learn is to take in and ponder viewpoints from a number of different paradigms. Do not be afraid to hear contrasting views to your own; in fact, encourage them.

## ALLOW OTHERS TO SAVE FACE

Whether student, peer, or other faculty member, no one likes to be wrong. Actually, many of us will often try to respond quickly and emotionally when we are told we are mistaken in an effort to prove why we are right. Worse yet, if we are embarrassed when we are wrong, we will react emotionally and defensively instead of admitting the sting of humiliation.

Avoid, if you can, singling out a student, faculty member, or peer as wrong in the company of others. If you need to have that conversation, it is best done in private. Better yet, you do not have to prove yourself right if you have accomplished the goal of setting the situation right.

## LISTEN TO OTHERS WHO THINK YOU ARE WRONG

If you are leading a class, school, or district (and doing so in a strong manner), you will always have a handful of people who may disagree with some aspect of your teaching or leading style. The easiest thing to do is simply "pooh-pooh" those who don't agree with what you are doing or saying.

The issue becomes that these critics of your way in doing things can offer you some important and needed feedback that may be very useful in problem solving or improvement. If everyone is giving you feedback that you are doing "an excellent job" and nobody tells you anything you can improve upon, you simply can't develop further professionally. Listen and ask those who disagree with you for feedback and further encourage this if it is done constructively. These people (including students) will teach you invariably more than others who simply are "back slappers" and pour compliments out without merit.

## A FEW WORDS ON LIKABILITY SPECIFIC TO STUDENTS

Most, if not all, of the suggestions above can also be applied to developing a positive relationship with students. Nevertheless, there are some specific items to think about when developing student interactions:

- *Respect your students:* As mentioned, respect is the key to getting students to like you. Respect is mutual; however, in the mind of a student, respect must be shown before it is demonstrated. If you say, "I must first get respect," someone has to model that first, and who will that be?
- *Understand what they go through:* Many of our students, in every district, come to school each day saddled with parents not able to put food on the table, domestic violence, or substance abuse issues that leave a child unable to find security and consistency in any place but school. Be aware that, just as some students have learning disabilities and limitations, many have just as significant environmental disabilities.
- *Know students live in many worlds:* Students live in a world with their peers and a world with adults. If you put an ear into their world without saying or doing anything, you can learn what truly is going on and how they react. This is opposed to what you are simply being told as secondhand hearsay by students which contains only what they want to hear.
- *Students are in a world almost entirely controlled by adults:* When you stop and think about it, adults control every aspect of a student's world: when they wake, who their teachers are, where they live, even when they can use the restroom. That being said, is it any wonder youth get frustrated?

  Giving your students as much control over some aspect of their school day as possible when appropriate will lead them to believe that you have trust in their budding abilities.

- *Avoid droning on and on:* Students don't like to hear us talk. Challenge students and allow them to experience learning using visual, auditory, and tactile skills. Less talking, more doing. Less lecturing, more fair discipline with logical consequences.
- *Recognize technology is their language:* This generation has been born into a world in which technology is the main form of communication. Therefore, it is vital that, as a part of your school climate, technology is utilized in an appropriate fashion in as many facets as possible. If you don't know technology, become familiar.
- *Look for success not failure:* This one seems simple but is valuable. Genuinely liking your students and their unique qualities and wanting them to succeed based on their strengths goes a very, very long way. It may seem obvious, but you may be surprised that there are educators who don't harbor these qualities in their professional attitude. They hear or read something about a student and their minds are made up.

Remember, it is not about forcing students to adhere to your way of teaching or a "one size fits all" approach. It is about tailoring education to the student. In fact, think of yourself as a tailor of pupils trying to make certain that what we provide them with fits their abilities and strengths. We cannot make them squeeze into a curriculum or model that simply does not fit their aptitudes or capacities.

## NOTES

1. Susan Cain, *Quiet: The Power of Introverts in a World That Can't Stop Talking* (New York: Crown Publishers, 2002).
2. Jennifer Cohen, "How Likeable Are You? Here Are 8 Ways You Can Improve Your Likeability at Work," *Forbes*, 7 April 2014, http://www.forbes.com/sites/jennifercohen/2014/04/07/how-likeable-are-you-here-are-8-ways-you-can-improve-your-likeability-at-work/#6dfa2a9f1596.
3. Donald T. Phillips, *Martin Luther King Jr. Lessons on Leadership: Inspiration and Wisdom for Challenging Times* (New York: Warner Books, 1999).

4. John Baldoni, "Managing Big Egos So the Entire Team Wins," *Harvard Business Review*, 19 February 2009, https://hbr.org/2009/02/managing-big-egos-so-the-entir (accessed 10 October 2016).

# *Chapter Four*

# Avoid Being a "Pushover," "Always Say Yes" Educator," "Host Gossiper," "Bully," or "Drama Mama/Papa"

> Bad communication gives us less room to grow.—Dr. Rowan Williams

In the world of education, one must be careful that the term "likable" does not mean weak, meek, or shallow. That being said, going too far in the other direction brings you into the realm of the very antithesis of being liked. Likability and effectiveness are, in fact, a delicate balance and a scaled concept rather than an absolute trait.

We are going to look at few different personality types in this chapter. Why? Because we need to look at what happens when you throw caution to the wind and avoid seeking a balance of the traits of productivity, effectiveness, and likability.

Please see figure 4.1 to gain a better understanding visually of the types of educators and the range that you will come into contact with on your educational career journey.

## THE "PUSHOVER" AND "ALWAYS SAY YES" EDUCATOR: IS "NO" A FOUR LETTER WORD?

As an educator, if you lean more toward the "likable" aspect of your personality, you will find the word "no" is one of the hardest words to say. Whether teacher, administrator, or paraprofessional, you may equate the word "no" with rejecting the other party, being difficult, or not falling into the category of a team player.

Guilt is usually what follows when saying no to anyone who asks if you are seeking to be well-liked. Therefore, it is best to develop a criterion of when to say no and when you may be willing to say yes and accept extra tasks or help another colleague.

### What Are Your Priorities?

If, as either a teacher or administrator, you make everything an emergency or priority in your decision making, then nothing will be. If you treat everything like a fire, you will soon run out of water as the fires continue to rage around you.

Ask yourself: what are my priorities? Priorities may change from time to time based on circumstance; however, they should serve as guide posts to your vision for your overall career and lifestyle.

A typical list of priorities may be (in order):

1. individual health (emotional and physical)
2. family (immediate)
3. extended family
4. career
5. friends
6. bills/caring for the house
7. community obligations
8. religious obligations

Of course, this is an example, and your priorities may be in a somewhat different order from these. What is important, however, is to know what your priorities are and remember them when two contradicting requests arrive in your lap. Having a blueprint for conflicting activities allows you to be able to have a rational versus emotional way of deciphering how you are going to handle varying and contrasting obligations.

If you say "yes" to everything, you will find yourself becoming increasingly resentful and burnt out (more on that later). Additionally, you wind up becoming a martyr and complaining about being taken advantage of or working too hard (and receive little to no sympathy).

## I Have Myself at the Bottom . . . Is That Okay?

Everyone's priorities, of course, are different. Based on your age, health, family, career obligations, and so on, they become more idiosyncratic to the individual. Many of those that tend to sway toward overly worrying about being liked find that they place themselves somewhere on the bottom of their priority list.

Everything they do or say is to put themselves at the very bottom of the list of priorities. They will do whatever in their career to get ahead and for the students/faculty as well as their family. Though well intentioned, what ends up happening is they unknowingly set a dangerous precedent. Let's go back to that priority list. Now imagine it as a percentage. You have 100 percent and must split that percentage according to your priorities:

1. individual health (emotional and physical) = __________ of 100%
2. family (immediate) = __________ of 100%
3. extended family = __________ of 100%
4. career = __________ of 100%
5. friends = __________ of 100%

6. bill/caring for the house = __________ of 100%
7. community obligations = __________ of 100%
8. religious obligations = __________ of 100%

Which of these items do you give the greatest percentage to? If you give 10 percent to something, some other obligation suffers. Water the garden of friendship with only 10 percent of the needed water and your friendships wither. Don't pay the bills and the collections agencies start calling.

Now, if you don't provide yourself time to do things for yourself as not just an educator, but as a parent, adult, spouse, and friend, you now have proportionally less than that 100 percent of you that must now be spread among the same priorities. Hence, you have even less of the greatest resource you have—yourself. You can now only give the respective percentages to those things you deem priorities in your life. See the danger? Putting yourself last actually sacrifices the quality you can provide to everything else that you hope to care for first.

## The "I Feel Bad" Connection

The role of any educator is exhausting. Often you play several roles such as of parent, educator, teacher, and social worker. In your career, you will see students and families in situations that one would never imagine and will work with children whose nightmares are all too real. For these situations, your empathy and compassion are very well needed and justified.

Then there are the other situations. The situations in which a peer or another stakeholder asks you to do something else. For instance, joining a committee, doing a favor, or extending a large courtesy to another, and you suddenly are left "feeling bad" because you did not fulfill someone else's expectations. You may believe that you are not a team player or beat yourself with an aching guilt.

Before "you feel bad," ask yourself:

- Is what they are asking possible?
- Am I doing this because I truly want to help them or because of my guilt?
- Am I being a team player or being taken advantage of?
- Is this best for my school, my class, my family?
- Am I sacrificing too much of my time to make their day slightly easier?
- Is this reciprocated?

### The Empty Sorry

How many times have you had a student (or your own child) say, "I am sorry"? They do not know what they are sorry about or why, yet they are saying it. Quite simply, they give an empty knee-jerk reaction because they think it is what the adult wants to hear.

Flash forward twenty years. As adults, we use the same tired "knee-jerk" paradigm for our world around us. When you encounter coworkers, fellow educators, and even at times students, you provide empty apologies. For instance, more than a few educators punctuate the ends of their sentences with, "oh . . . I am sorry (for fill in the blank __________)."

Unless you have wronged someone and are sincere of your doing so, do not give an empty apology. Hollow apologies make one seem like a pushover, lacking genuineness. Conversely, this makes you seem weaker and can create irritation in those who recognize this nervous habit.

## THE HOST GOSSIPER

We all know these persons; they are in the faculty room and in the hallowed halls of every school building. They are the gossipers. They hold court every day to convey the latest tidbits of scandal that are unique to each school. They have their cabinet members who hang on their every word and add their own spin to the game of "telephone" that distorts the information even further.

If (and when) you encounter the gossiper, it becomes a litmus test of your ability to be trusted. If others see you talking about others, then they know, inevitably, that you deem it safe to talk behind another's back. Put another way, if they are gossiping about someone to you, it is a good chance that you will be next on the chopping block when your head is turned.

### How to Avoid Being Sucked into the Gossip Whirlpool

- Avoid the places where gossip dwells such as the faculty room, hallways, social media sites, and soccer fields.
- Make it a rule in your interactions to defend those who are not present.
- Do not give others a reason to gossip about you. Be straightforward and honest and do not try to stir drama when it is not needed.

## THE CASE OF THE DRAMA MAMAS AND PAPAS

These are the people that truly believe the sky is falling at every turn within a school. They fear change and look for any subtle cue that things may be going south and then sound the proverbial alarm.

The goal? Try to get everyone else to panic and wring their hands along with them. If the case of misery loves company is true, their mantra is drama likes company as well.

### How to Avoid Becoming a Drama Mama or Papa

The following are some ideas to help from getting ensnared in a web of drama:

- Recognize these dramatic people operate primarily out of emotion and not logic. This means that when you address this issue, do so out of logic to bring them back to reality.
- Know these people do not like change. Change is equal to anxiety because these people like to hold steadfast to what they are comfortable with. When they get out of this bubble, they can react emotionally or even explosively. Prepare these people for change and give them as much information as they are comfortable with to handle the new situation.
- Do not feed into the emotion. Dramatic people are often very emotional and are seeing if anyone else gets sucked into their drama as well. To make an analogy, if you are fearful of flying, you will listen very attentively to the pilot, and if he is calm, you are calmer. If he/she has any slight hint of nervousness in their voice, the person afraid of flying will panic. Think of yourself as the aviator of those you work with and pilot accordingly.
- Watch out for passive-aggressive behaviors: these people create drama and show anger in an indirect manner. They may not seem angry . . . but don't turn your back. Address these people directly and do not fall into the trap of their innocuously placing hurdles in the way of your goals and expectations because they do not like to express anger in a direct and effective manner.

## THE BULLY

Often we think of students bullying their peers when we discuss the concepts of harassment, intimidation, or bullying. Don't be fooled, though; this same behavior plays out in all manners of peer and parent, as well as student, interactions. It may appear to be more covert than the pushing and taunting of adults, however.

If you are to be effective with any bully, it must start early. Bullies are used to directly and aggressively pushing their agenda. They will intentionally push their boundaries to see how far and what they can get. This being said, often they are given what they want or will take it by causing a scene or by the force of their strong personalities.

Being productive means setting definite and strong boundaries early and often. A faculty member or parent that knows but does not respect limits of how far they can push will stop only when they are forced. If they cannot "take a mile" with each step, only then will they take more measured and appropriate actions.

The issue becomes when you don't stop them immediately in their tracks. Often we confuse giving in with accommodating these persons. When you do this, they take a step forward, and metaphorically you take a step backward each time they do. Eventually, due to policy, your values, or frustration, you stop them and set your limits. It is too late then as they become angry and furious at your waffling based on your accommodating to their past demands and now not doing so.

If you are not certain how to excuse yourself and have a conversation at a later time when these persons "demand" you to immediately meet at their whim, please see the "Open-Door Policy" section discussed earlier in this book.

## "THE BACK SLAPPER"

These are the educators (though they pervade every field) that are always trying to get everyone to like them by saying nice things to everyone. Yet these empty compliments are never anything genuine or specific. They tell students or faculty, "You are the best," "You are my favorite," "You are a great student/teacher," and so forth.

Now, while there is nothing wrong with complimenting, the difficulty is when it comes across as lacking genuine quality. If everyone is the best, essentially no one is the best; if everyone is your favorite, no one is your favorite; and if everyone is great, what does that mean? Also, if someone is quick to give inflated compliments, the pendulum can quickly swing to the very opposite extreme just as easily.

Rather, be specific with your praise and careful. Know the person or student you are speaking to and take the time to tailor your compliments specifically. Don't rush on your words of encouragement; make them specific and sincere. Less is more: a kind word is better than an overexaggeration.

## "THE PROCRASTINATOR"

This is the person that is perpetually by the proverbial water cooler of your school, namely the faculty room. They are not the gossiper; in fact, they are really quite pleasant. They are the ones, however, that just has a hard time getting started with their day, their week, their year. They are chronically late for everything or "miss" their obligations to the educational team.

They may be "burned out" and looking for a buddy to join them in pleasant conversation. There is certainly a time for this; however, be cautious because the idle time you spend may be more than you have and they will suck out whatever time you give them.

Excuse yourself gracefully as, again, time is a commodity that you cannot share too much of with this person. If you give them twenty-three hours, they will want twenty-four.

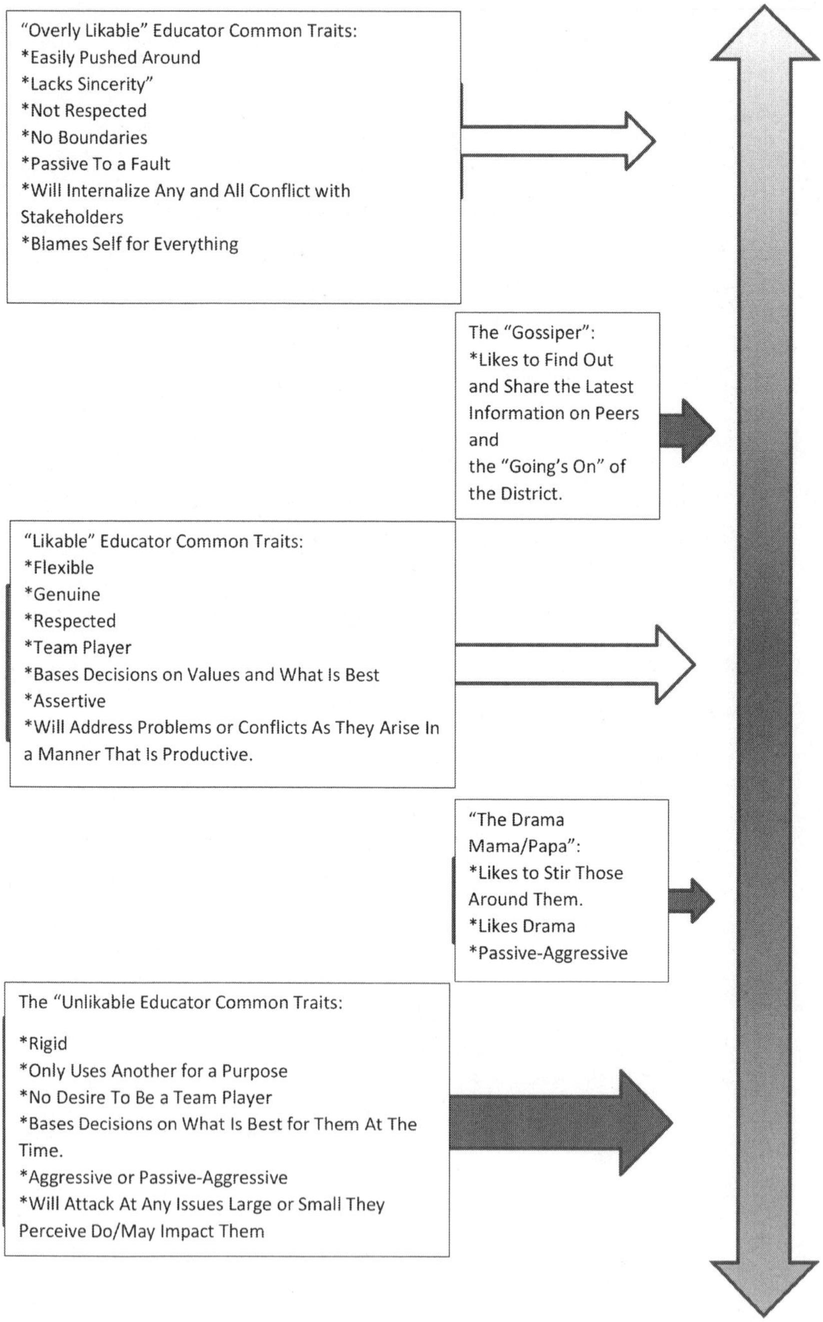


**Figure 4.1. Types of Educators**

*Chapter Five*

# What is Important to You? What Are Your Base Values?

> Intelligence plus character—that is the goal of true education.—
> Dr. Martin Luther King Jr.

Schools can be difficult places to navigate. As politics, policies, and leadership shift, so can the climate, values, and vision of the school district. Some leaders may have values that bend what you consider ethically or morally viable. From this, you will see two types of faculty: those that "follow orders" dutifully and others that stand up for their opinions and beliefs and don't stretch their beliefs to conform to whatever the school climate dictates.

Values are a very tricky arena to tackle. The truth is you are buffeted by a number of factors that can easily distort or blur your vision if not overly cautious. The variety of obligations and stakeholders involved in a district can further muddy the waters of your decision making. As the proverbial ship sways, your eyes on the true horizon of your values must remain steadfast.

## "I WAS JUST FOLLOWING ORDERS"

Many of us try to assuage our guilt by saying "we are just following orders" when a superior asks us to do something that directly contradicts our values or ethics.

If something contradicts your values, you cannot be genuine, productive, or effective by simply "going along with it." If you follow it simply because "well . . . everyone is doing it," remember, it is still wrong if it is outside the bounds of your personal values or your professional ethics regardless of your attempts to rationalize it.

To avoid this, you must establish your own firm boundaries with what you understand to be your own personal values and code of ethics. If you do not do so early, you will eventually get sucked into a cesspool of some situation you disagree with inherently. If you go along directly against your better judgment, it will only serve to disintegrate your morale and overall school climate.

Taking the idea of "just following orders" to an extreme is the infamous 1961 Milgram experiment in which a random group of people were selected and told they were doing an experiment on "memory and learning."[1] They then were instructed to "teach" word pair lessons to the "student" (who was only acting as the subject). When the "subject" got an answer incorrect, the participant was to give them, initially, mild shocks.

The "shock" went from a scale of 75 volts (moderate) to 450 (which was beyond severe). The shocks were, in fact, fake, and the person acting as the subject was only feigning receiving the jolt. Nevertheless, the so-called teacher did not know this and was advised to "just follow orders" and continued to administer gradually higher levels of shock.

The result? Despite most "teachers" feeling uncomfortable doing so, all forty subjects obeyed and provided the false shocks up to 300 volts (labeled between Strong and Danger Severe Shock). More disturbingly, twenty-five of the forty subjects continued to give shocks until the maximum level of 450 volts (above Danger Severe Shock) was achieved. "Just following orders" and not using our own judgment and conscience can be an extremely scary prospect indeed.

## THE "PUT YOUR HEAD ON THE PILLOW AT NIGHT" TEST

Any system with large numbers of people develops a complex web of relationships and its own idiosyncratic political climate. There will be those who try to get ahead in your district by any means possible. They will lie, cheat, steal, or employ varying devious means of getting what they want.

"Kissing up," gossiping, and development of cliques all naturally evolve in many school settings. Many times in this carousel of interaction, you will find things happening that just don't seem fair, equitable, or just.

A simple test, however, to establish if you are preserving your own integrity is, "Can I put my head on my pillow at night?" If you have pangs of guilt, you may indeed be violating your own belief system or code of morality.

Ask yourself:

1. Did I do the right thing today? If not, what would I do different?
2. If I had to explain the situation to my mother/father/mentor/child, would I be proud?
3. If I were to go to court, could I defend my actions?
4. Does this align with my family and cultural sense of what is right?

## A REVIEW OF BASIC VALUE ATTRIBUTES

### 1. Honesty

- Are you being honest with yourself in this situation?
- Do you need to rationalize what you are doing to make it "fit" into your definition of what is right? Do you find yourself saying, "Well, everyone else is doing it. I am just following the orders of the administration or board"?
- Is the situation being judged honestly, rationally, or emotionally?
- Does it pass the above "Can I Put My Head on My Pillow Tonight" Test?

### 2. Confidentiality

- Can faculty, parents, or students count on you to keep what they tell you in confidence?
- Do you defend those that are not within your immediate presence? Do you not speak ill of those not in your immediate presence?
- If you break someone's confidence, is it to protect them or someone else in some significant way? Or just for gossip?

### 3. Realness

Many of us put on the hat of the professional when we are at work. Of course, it is extremely important to be a professional in all aspects of your job. Also, however, people, including your students, must see you as a genuine person.

How can you be more real?

- They should know that you are not perfect and that you can, and will, admit and own up to your mistakes.
- They should know that you recognize most people prioritize family over work if push comes to shove.

- You have values and opinions that remain steadfast and don't wax and wane with who you are speaking with or your situation.
- You laugh at yourself and at your flaws.
- You are honest and can be trusted to keep confidence with others.
- Do you do what you say and say what you do? Are you the kind of person that tells your faculty to follow a specific set of rules, guidelines, or values and then displays the complete opposite in your own career or life?

### 4. Competence

There is a terrible saying that states, "Those who can't, teach." The saying is rooted in the obvious idea that those who are not capable teach others in a hope that they will have some investment in those who are able to reach those levels of success.

This is a horrible and destructive notion. Nevertheless, there may be some thread of truth in that if you are going to lead a class or a school and are not willing to prove or try to do it. You must be competent in most areas in which you are leading. Otherwise, you find yourself leading from behind.

Learn and be up-to-date on as much in your chosen educational vocation as possible. Learn new techniques, innovative technologies, and trends. Read up in journals, the Internet, and professional development both in and out of your respective district. If you don't know or understand some aspect of your role, learn it—be a lifelong learner.

### 5. Creativity and Logic

There is a time and a place for both thinking inside the box as well as needing to go outside of the box. Try to balance both of these skills and do not demean the value of either or both in yourself or others.

### 6. Appreciation

Yes, every student, staff, teacher, administrator has a job to do. However, it is important that you provide appreciation when it is warranted and regularly. This school climate trickles down (and hopefully up) throughout the educational ladder.

## WHAT IS YOUR GOAL STATEMENT(S) FOR YOUR CAREER?

Many organizations have an overarching vision or mission that can be used it as the simplest template of what is acceptable or unacceptable to their ultimate goal as an organization or business.

Ideally, this statement should stay unwavering despite what moral and ethical tsunamis are thrown your way. Rest assured, in your career, your ethics, morals, and beliefs will be tested at one point or another.

For further information and to tailor your value-drive statement, see figure A.2 in the appendix for a better means to prioritize your value-driven goal statements.

### To Develop Your Career Statement

1. What is it that you want to accomplish over the next five years?
2. If you had one wish in your career, what would it look like?
3. Does this statement meet with your personal values and morals?
4. Simple is better. This is the one standing statement that you will fall back upon. It is not specifics; it is the framework for which to build your career goals.
5. Is it practical and attainable?

6. Is the statement you set inspirational to you? If it does not ignite a fire for you, how will it carry you forward in your career?
7. Is your mission in line with the district vision, goals, and mission?

## Begin with an Eye Toward the End

Imagine after your long and storied educational career, you have hundreds of beloved colleagues and your family at your retirement. What would they say? What would you like to be the highlights of your career? How would former students, the community, and every colleague at each level of the school system describe you? When you get up to speak, what do you say?

Now, you have the ending of your mission. You are at point A (now) and you know point B (the end). The vital element is how to connect the two. That very connecting line becomes the vocational mission ahead.

## NOTE

1. Wolfgang Frindte and Daniel Geschke, "Stanley Milgram: Obedience to Authority. An Experiment View. Harper & Row: New York 1974, 224 S. (dt. Das Milgram-Experiment. Zur Gehorsamsbereitschaft Gegenüber Autoritäten. Rowohlt Verlag: Reinbek Bei Hamburg 1974, 256 S.)," *Klassiker Der Sozialwissenschaften* (2016).

*Chapter Six*

# Recognizing Culture in the Nature of Likability

> Culture makes people understand each other better. And if they understand each other better in their soul, it is easier to overcome the economic and political barriers. But first they have to understand that their neighbour is, in the end, just like them, with the same problems, the same questions.—Paulo Coelho

If you are a rule follower, like myself, you will be very careful as you traverse the world around you. A "rule follower" is diligent to make certain that they do not step over the bounds of the vast array of laws, policies, and boundaries that surround the world of work, society, and community that they inhabit. It is pretty simple to find what the regulations are in any aspect of the setting. Usually, there is a law, statute, or policy that dictates almost every aspect of the rules and the subsequent consequence or punishment for just about everything. Look in a book or on the web and you find the answer.

Often, the proverbial "elephant in the room" that plays as the background music of every interaction is that of culture. Culture is the one aspect of the world that often does not have defined boundaries. Rather, it has many shades of gray that straddle the line of what may be appropriate, what may be offensive, and what may be stereotypical in nature. Yet, without knowledge of and sensitivity to cultures, you risk being insensitive or, worse yet, harassing to the parents and faculty that you interact with every day.

Reference.com indicates that there are an "estimated 5,000 to 6,000 cultures" around the globe.[1] The website notes, however, that this is a loose number because they can only base the count on the number of languages in the world and some cultures, unfortunately, "dwindle due to globalization spreading different systems and beliefs."

There are many articles that you can search on the Internet that indicate just how contrasting American culture can be compared to those around the rest of the world. Before you read this chapter, it may be useful to see what your level of comprehension is of cultural awareness areas. If you turn to figure A.2 in the appendix, it will provide you some questions that will help in beginning this discussion.

The following are areas that may provide you with some guidelines for working with persons of the varying cultures you will meet. Remember, however, that cultural diversity means that these areas are not concretely defined roles. Rather, it means that these are simply guideposts to give a deeper thought of what it means to live in a multicultural as well as diverse and ever-flattening world. It is a fine line between being sensitive and stereotyping.

- *You don't know what you don't know:* Often, you can violate cultural norms without even knowing it. For example, if you are working with devoutly Orthodox Jewish women or Muslim women, your first instinct may be to shake their hands. They indicate they will not shake your hand or turn away. Your first thoughtmay be did I do something offensive or are they slighting me? As it turns out, Orthodox or Muslim women are not allowed to make any physical contact with a man with whom they are not married. You may say, "I did not know I violated a cultural norm. I was just trying to be friendly." Hence a moment of discomfort may pervade all parties in the room.

- *Ask questions and learn:* Most people of varying cultures will be happy to discuss their culture with you as well as the reasons for why they do what they do. Learn and experience other cultures as much as possible and keep an open mind. Go to cultural festivals, eat in restaurants, travel, listen, and learn.
- *Personal space is cultural:* Often we teach students about being aware of another peer's personal space. We think of personal space as an absolute, but it is not and is culturally based. In the United States, we tend to be more sensitive about our personal space and prefer a "buffer" between ourselves and others. In Latin American, Hispanic, and Italian American cultures, there is a tendency to be accepting of less personal space. Why do you need to know this as an educator?

  Hace you ever know a person that is a "close talker"? You may be more comfortable with this type of person if they match your cultural paradigm. The problem is that other faculty may encounter this as aggressive and offensive and react to the body language or, worse yet, turn away and ignore the person.
- *Eye contact:* If you are teaching a child social skills in the United States, we will often associate eye contact with listening and being polite. Yet, in certain Asian, Native American, Latin, and African cultures, that very same eye contact is considered rude and aggressive. Western European cultures, however, adopt similar eye-contact tacit rules to what we utilize here. If you see a parent or faculty member break glance with you, do not assume that they are not listening, are being deceitful, or are acting rude. Do not continue to encourage continued eye contact if you are not certain that this is a cultural difference. Rudeness is a matter of culture and mutual understanding.
- *A simple touch can step over the line:* Often, we are taught that illicit touch in the work world is sexual harassment. However, light touch is often associated with friendliness. Yet, it is important to note that in the Orthodox Jewish and Muslim cultures, it is

considered inappropriate to touch in any way a person of the opposite gender who is not your family member or spouse. This includes handshakes, a stroke of the arm, or a pat on the back.

- *A weak handshake means a weak person:* Many males in the United States have been taught that a firm handshake is the sign of a strong and confident person. When we meet a parent or interview a potential faculty member, we might think something like, "That handshake was like a limp fish." It will then taint how you see a parent or potential employee. In some Asian cultures, a strong handshake is considered rude. Also, being the first to let go of the embrace may be rude, and in other cultures, it is considered inappropriate to shake hands at all (sometimes bowing is used in its place). Best response: put out your hand and await their response and then mirror what they are doing.
- *Know your holidays:* The New Jersey Department of Education recognizes more than one hundred holidays of varying cultures throughout the academic year.[2] Now, it is not possible to know all the holidays (major and minor) that are celebrated throughout a year. However, one should know the major holidays for each major culture. This is especially true if you work in a school district that has a particularly high population of one culture or another.
- *Nuclear families are not the norm:* In today's society, families come in a spectrum of sizes and types: single-parent, same-sex parents, foster, and a whole host of other types of families exist. One can elicit offense by only catering to or recognizing one type of family in letters you send home or on a district website. Recognize that we are not just educating various types of pupils but also diverse kinds of families as well.
- *Avoid topics of controversy:* As we highlighted earlier, avoid politics and religion. This is especially true when you are dealing with cultural thoughtfulness and ways of life that are unfamiliar to you. When you enter the world of "hot button" topics as well

as the realm of humor, the aspects of culture and sensitivity get quite murky. Avoid these topics and it will keep you from having to save an embarrassing moment and/or offending someone inadvertently.

- *Do not think of culture as only global . . . but also regional:* In the Midwest and South, people tend to be more friendly. In the Northeast and New England, persons have a tendency toward being more reserved. In fact, journalist Colin Woodard, in his book *American Nations: A History of Eleven Rival Cultures in North America*, states that "we are a country divided into eleven separate cultures in regions throughout the U.S."[3] Regardless, if one subscribes to this theory, it is important to know the cultural makeup of your community to avoid being culturally insensitive.
- *Have a good character education and anti-bullying program:* In a world that is brightened and characterized by the freedom to celebrate who you are and your culture; racism, bias, and bullying may, undoubtedly, still rear their ugly heads. This becomes especially true when you put a population of malleable children in an environment in which they are all expected to collaborate and work together.

  A good character education and anti-bullying program that includes a strong cultural diversity component will teach an invaluable lesson of recognizing, accepting, and embracing all cultures. Programs correlated with historical figures of varying cultures can also represent a good cross-curricular lesson of character education as well as history.
- *Be careful what subtleties are in your statement(s):* Again, this can surprise you. For instance, when we adopted my daughter from South Korea, we questioned the adoption director if she was sure that the reason my daughter's adoption was delayed was due to her having pink eye. Innocuous question, right? Wrong! What she heard was a questioning of her very integrity. What she heard was, "Are you lying to me or not being honest

about her having pink eye?" We deeply offended her by just asking a simple (culturally appropriate) question that really had a deeper (unintended) meaning in a divergent culture.

- *Make community connections:* The public school system is part of a community. Having an understanding of the community around you is vital. As the school leader, reaching out to culturally based community organizations can help you better understand the community and also be proactive in putting a positive step toward good multicultural community relations. Visiting community, cultural, and religious centers may go a long way toward building bridges.
- *Education isn't only learned in formal schooling and in colleges/universities:* Different cultures place diverse emphasis on formalized education. Some cultures find it a more vital aspect of one's life. For others, direct firsthand experiences are more important. Just because you as an educator place a high emphasis on formalized education does not mean you can expect everyone to have the same priorities or expectations that you harbor.

As the world continues to flatten, our students will continue to be citizens of an ever-changing and diverse world. That being said, we are also more and more involved in all aspects of the globe as the Internet makes the earth accessible with a few simple clicks of a mouse. Therefore, we must become global citizens and develop not just the language of technological fluency, but also cultural fluency as well.

- *Everyone has a culture:* Many of us neglect our own cultural biases and beliefs. The fact is everyone has a cultural background, and therefore you have a cultural bias that tints your relational, vocational, and political views on everything. Therefore, be certain to question everything when you believe your opinion is absolute. Try to understand the other's view before you impact another with what you believe to be your opinion or "what is right." Always be cautious in the area of right and wrong in regard to the realm of culture and opinions.

## THE AMERICAN CULTURE IS A CULTURE IN ITSELF

Being an American is its own cultural microcosm. For instance, the following represent a stereotypical paradigm of the overall cultural values of the majority of Americans.

### American Culture

*We like change:* As Americans we see change and advancement as positive things. We talk about advancing as a "good thing." We are constantly trying to progress and improve ourselves. One only has to look at the glut of self-help books or the latest smartphone apps to know we are not generally comfortable with the status quo.

### Contrasting Cultural Value of Some Other Countries

*Other cultures prefer stability and tradition:* If you go to other countries or look at other cultures, advancement and change are not necessarily always positive qualities. Rather a strong adherence to tradition and keeping the stability of guidelines that have gone back hundreds and, in some cases, thousands of years is preferred. Change is therefore sharply guarded against and will be pushed back accordingly.

### How It Impacts Your Educational Conversation with Students/Parents/Faculty

If you are one who expects rapid change in your school or parental culture, recognize that there is a level of tradition or comfort in the past. Respect the past and present and that all change is stressful regardless of the positive or negative connotation it provides.

## American Culture

*Rush for time:* Americans tend to be very time-oriented and conscious. We have all heard the expressions "Time is money," "Your time is valuable," "Give the gift of time." This leads us to stingily restrict our time or rush each day to get the most done in the smallest and most efficient amount of time possible.

## Contrasting Cultural Value of Some Other Countries

*Importance of connection:* Time is not measured with getting things done or being equitable. It is more important to focus on family and social interactions. Therefore, a limited amount of time as Americans is our primary focus. Other cultures are focused on trying to build human relationships.

## How It Impacts Your Educational Conversation with Students/Parents/Faculty

*If you are attempting to get something done quickly with others:* Recognize that if you hurry this interaction in hopes of seeing results, you may be working against yourself. Rather, know that others will not trust or work with you unless you have emotionally joined and clicked with them. Without a strong bond, you cannot make a withdrawal from their relational account.

## American Culture

*We want equality and fairness in all of our interactions:* Our culture comes from a perspective of "liberty and justice for all." One of the most important elements in the very fabric that weaves through the American cultural framework is that of making certain we are all treated fairly and equally. We have fought hard to be certain of this most basic, vital, and inalienable right.

## Contrasting Cultural Value of Some Other Countries

*Other countries have a hierarchy system:* This could be based on age. For example some cultures recognize those that elders or certain professions may have a higher status then others. In India and Pakistan, for instance, there is a caste system, which is a means of socially stratifying persons based on occupation and wealth. Gender is also a contrast in some cultures in terms of one sex having hierarchical roles over another.

Keep in mind, though you may have disagreements or contrasting viewpoints, it is important to respect and recognize long-held historical values.

## How It Impacts Your Educational Conversation with Students/Parents/Faculty

*Equality:* Your perception of gender or socioeconomic beliefs to "get ahead" may be met with resistance in some cases. You may try to push for a certain issue, but behind the scenes, you may be pushing up against a cultural barrier that you were hitherto unaware of.

## American Culture

*As Americans we seek to be individuals:* We strive to stand out from others, seek our own freedom to make choices, and work toward being the very best as individuals as far as our capitalist edicts will allow. Competition is encouraged as is individualism.

## Contrasting Cultural Value of Some Other Countries

*In other cultures, it is not about the individual:* In fact, it is frowned upon to consider yourself outside of your social group. It is the village, not the person, emphasized, and it is the group that matters more than the individual. Complimenting a person may be met with modest embarrassment.

## How It Impacts Your Educational Conversation with Students/Parents/Faculty

This is a vital notion to realize if you have an issue of discord with an individual; recognize that some cultures consider this an affront to the group as a whole. Individualism is less often stressed, so the culture looks toward what is for the best of the whole rather than that of the one. The group will also vehemently defend the individual in the name of the group.

## American Culture

*Our culture tends to be less formal by many standards:* We do not usually have relatively elaborate, structured routines in terms of eating, drinking, or holidays. This is because we all have numerous manners of celebration due, in part, to our multitude of cultures and nationalities that we have "melted into one pot."

## Contrasting Cultural Value of Some Other Countries

*Other cultures have elaborate traditions and ceremonies that are idiosyncratic to their particular cultures and go back hundreds or thousands of years:* These are accompanied by a great deal of formality, pomp, circumstance, and tradition that serve to bond generation to generation.

## How It Impacts

As may cultures have traditions and established routines that are more formalized than some of those typically attributed to our culture it is vital that we ask questions in regards to those practices we are not familiar with, so as not to offend others. We can only follow rules, boundaries, and customs that we are aware of. When we are not we tread on very delicate ice. Therefore, it is far better to question and ask than to offend and apologize.

### American Culture

*We tend to be direct in our communication:* We are a "mean what you say . . . say what you mean" culture for the most part. This can be interpreted in some cultures as rude or intrusive.

### Contrasting Cultures

*Other cultures tend to be more reserved:* Certain topics are taboo to bring up immediately. Additionally, a level of conversation and relationship needs to be established before you delve into a topic that can be sensitive in nature.

### How It Impacts Your Educational Conversation with Students/Parents/Faculty

*Sometimes we expect an emotional or immediate reaction when we discuss an issue with another:* If we tell a parent that their child is going to be suspended, we expect some demonstrative reaction. If we state that you are not doing your job correctly, we anticipate an expressive retort to demonstrate that your occupation, and my criticism of it, is vital to you. Just because you do not get an immediate emotional response from the other party does not mean it is any less relevant in any particular cultural model.

## GENERATIONAL GAPS ARE CULTURAL GAPS TOO

Recognize that, whether you are a veteran educator or a relatively young one, you have a generational culture. According to the *Fairleigh Dickinson University Winter Magazine* of 2005[4] there are some very real contrasts in workplace attitudes between persons of just a few decades apart. Of course, these are generalities but can be helpful in understanding.

- Generation Z (2000–present): Are technologically in tune and do not remember times when technology and the Internet were not a central part of life. They tend to be more comfortable with computer/Internet-based forms of communication, they like to find how their job and lifestyle can intersect, and they can be adept at self-motivating.

Interacting with this generation: Prefer short, technologically centered communications. Important to demonstrate how your role as an educator plays an important part in the larger community dynamic.

- Millennials/Generation Y (1980–2000): Tend to want more flexibility in their work environment, are comfortable with working in a team setting, see themselves as part of a larger picture, focus more on home and family than strictly vocational goals.

  Interacting with this generation: Team-building activities as well as committees and small learning groups are a strength and a preferred manner of development (generally). Remember to stress that you understand family will generally take precedence over vocation.

- Generation X (1965–1979): Tend to value a balance of work and family life; see themselves as a marketable resource and may shift employers accordingly. They tend to be results-oriented and are the initial rise of those that were born into the generation of technology competency skills.

  Interacting with this generation: Important (especially in this generation group) to let them know that they are appreciated and their services are, indeed, a respected commodity. Outcome-based measures are generally a good means of helping to understand progress and make suggestions with this groups' analytical decision making.

- Baby Boomers (1946–1964): In the workplace, this generation is known to be oriented toward goals and achievements. They can be fiercely independent and have a strong work ethic and loyalty to one or very few trusted employers.

Interacting with this generation: Stressing appreciation of loyalty and recognition of contribution and hard work is vital in keeping these employees happy.

## NOTES

1. "Cultures & Traditions." Reference.com. Web. 08 Nov. 2016.
2. New Jersey Department of Education, "List of Religious Holidays Permitting Pupil Absence from School," http://www.state.nj.us/educaton/genfo/holiday.htm (accessed 29 September 2006).
3. Colin Woodard, *American Nations: A History of the Eleven Rival Regional Cultures of North America* (New York: Viking, 2011).
4. Greg Hammill, "Mixing and Managing Four Generations of Employees," *Fairleigh Dickinson University Magazine*, Winter/Spring 2005, http://www.fdu.edu/newspubs/magazine/05ws/generations.htm (accessed 28 August 2016).

*Chapter Seven*

# Being a Good/Better Listener

> Being a good listener, you are able to connect with others on more levels and develop stronger, deeper relationships.—John C. Maxwell

## OPEN YOUR EARS . . . CLOSE YOUR MOUTH

Often we are too busy talking to listen. We encourage our students to learn by listening to us and yet we find it difficult to close our own mouths to listen to others.

The first, and foremost, rule is we have to simply stop talking to listen and learn. If you think this is an easy task, listen to how many of your colleagues are talking at your next meeting. Most spout opinions, suggestions, or complaints. How many, however, are just simply listening?

This, in many cases, is what separates productive and effective people from the alternative.

## DON'T THINK . . . JUST LISTEN

If you are thinking of what to say next, your grocery list, or what happened last week, you are not listening. You are definitely hearing, but hearing and listening are very different contrasting activities.

How do you know you are hearing and not listening? The test is when you cannot recall any or only scant details of a conversation you just had or are currently having. This can happen when the conversation in your head about the events in your life is so loud that you cannot hear that of the other person.

## DON'T INTERRUPT

Count how many times you interrupt a conversation with a fellow educator, parent, or student. The amount that you interrupt conversely equates with how well you are listening.

## COUNT THE "YOU, ME, I'S"

If you're using the words "me and I" in the majority of a conversation, you are shifting the balance of the conversation to yourself. If you're saying "you," then you are indeed focusing the discussion to your speaker.

## LEARN ABOUT OTHERS . . . WANT TO LEARN ABOUT OTHERS

The easiest way to be a good listener is to want to sincerely listen and know about others. If you want to know about them and recognize that everyone no matter their age or role in your life can teach you something, you will naturally be a good communicator. Learning about their likes, dislikes, family, opinions, culture, and experiences enriches your life and makes you a better listener just by your simple motivation to do so.

## THIS MEANS ASKING QUESTIONS TOO

If you ask questions, you will learn more about someone obviously. Asking close-ended questions that require only a simple "yes" or "no" response, however, vastly limits what you can and will learn, as will rote questions on weather or similar routine questions.

Rather, asking questions that are open ended allows a person to elaborate more and provides you with further material to ask a follow-up (or several follow-up) questions to guide you to even deeper insight about others.

Start questions with:

- "Tell me about . . ."
- "Can you explain more about . . ."
- "What made you decide to . . ."
- "I am curious about . . ."
- "Tell me your opinion on . . ."

## REMEMBER THAT "OPEN-DOOR POLICY" EARLIER?

It cannot be stressed enough that you can't "always be on" to listen to others. Recognize the amount of concentration and work that such an action takes. In doing so, honor those you communicate with by providing them the absolute honesty that you are (or are not) ready to have a conversation.

When you are tired, hungry, sleepy, overworked, or stressed, don't try to force a conversation. When you are listening half-heartedly, you cannot genuinely give the gift of being present and the presence of your time.

## THE SIMPLE NOD

Just nodding when someone is talking gives them the permission to continue to talk to you. They are receiving a subtle message that you are listening and approving the continued flow of their conversation. A simple soft "uh-huh" provides a similar parallel verbal communication.

## AVOID CONFUSING TECHNOLOGY FOR CLEAR COMMUNICATION

Most of us use technology for every aspect of our lives. It is hard to imagine a time when we did not have a smartphone providing us a constant and steady stream of communication to the world around us every second of every day.

It only takes watching teenagers in a mall texting each other as they are shoulder to shoulder walking along. Quality communication has been replaced with a "junk food" type communication that is quick and easy, though not often fulfilling in its interactional discourse.

Technological communication can be misunderstood and manipulated and lacks the accompanying nonverbal and verbal inflections and personal contact. In short, avoid it if you are striving to make a warm and personal connection. Use it, however, if you need to expedite, be efficient, or document a statement you wish to make.

## LEANING AHEAD

If you lean away from a person (such as leaning back in your office or classroom chair), you give them a nonverbal impression of lacking interest. It may not be readily apparent to either the listener or the recipient in a verbal fashion. That being said, however, the nonverbal impression is that you are "repelled" because your body language indicates you are retracting from the individual you are speaking with.

Rather, if you lean forward, you are showing a sincere interest in what the person is saying. This still means keeping in mind personal space; however, it is an important minute detail that will aid in other's feeling comfortable that you are listening and are vested in connecting with them.

## IT MEANS WANTING TO LISTEN

This may seem obvious but if you do not have an interest in hearing or listening you will find what others have to say boring and mundane. If you do not care to hear their opinions, thoughts, or what they value, then you will just be doing superficial listening. Hence, you will "hear" what they are saying but not "see" what they are talking about. If you know the answers to everything, you will not want to hear the questions or alternate ideas that another is offering.

Listening, hence, is about caring about the other's viewpoint as much (if not more) than your own. It is about silencing the voice inside of you that screams to be heard and realizing that everyone around you can teach you something if you just listen.

## IN SUMMARY

The ideas of listening cannot be overstated. The tactics are simple, seemingly, but "the devil is in the details." It is often very minor changes that make a separation between a good listener and someone who passively hears what is being told to them.

Remember, that most people can tell if you are listening or just appeasing them. Those that don't see this initially will eventually recognize you as not a good listener if they are fairly astute communicators themselves. They will be then quick to tell others, "Yeah, he/she is nice, but they never listen to what I/we are saying to them."

Unsure if you are still a good listener? Ask yourself how many times someone talks to you and a few minutes later you say, "Now . . . what did they say to me?" If this happens more often than not, you have an answer. Get working on those listening skills.

*Chapter Eight*

# Fear and Avoiding Becoming a "Pro"crastinator

> Procrastination is like a credit card: it's a lot of fun until you get the bill.—Christopher Parker

As more and more is expected of administrators and educators throughout the country, it is very easy to become overwhelmed with the abundance of job responsibilities that are stacked upon you.

It becomes simpler on some days to just stick your head in a hole like the notorious ostrich trying to escape the stresses and reality of your vocational life. As expectations and deadlines swirl around you like a tornado, in the end they can catch up with you and will carry you to a place where you are buried so deep in obligations and responsibilities that you cannot see straight as to what to do next.

## RECOGNIZE NOT EVERYTHING IS AN EMERGENCY AND ALL OBLIGATIONS ARE NOT CREATED EQUAL

Some of us tend to be more sensitive and reactive to stress and commitments in our occupational roles. If you tend to be anxious and regard every task as critical, you must triage and realize that if you do not have some means of prioritizing everything, you will have a problem with finishing anything.

## GO WITH THE MOST DIFFICULT TASK(S) FIRST

If you are like most people, you push away the most difficult or distasteful tasks that you have to do to the back burner. Additionally, you push the thought of it to the back of your mind (or so you think). Yet, it is akin to trying to outrun a train that is getting faster and faster; eventually it will overtake you.

Finishing the most challenging activities you dread first has two important components:

1. You are at your best and have the most energy to deal with the task that requires the most of your abilities.
2. When the task that you dreaded is done, you can now be free to deal with the rest of the day with a clearer head.

## PLAY THE "WHAT IF" GAME

Sometimes when we think of a task or confront an issue, we are simply afraid to do so. In turn, the issue becomes bigger and scarier and takes on a life of its own.

Ask yourself the "what if" as the worst-case scenario of the potential problem. Think about, challenge, and carry this problem beyond the possible end result to the greatest potential worst-case scenario.

Now, think of what potential solutions would be at your disposal in this case. Debate with your mind: How can I solve this? What if *all* goes wrong? Then what?

By exaggerating the problem, you can now pull back and see the issue as much more manageable and minor than that of the huge potential concern that your brain has fabricated.

## BREAK DOWN INSTEAD OF BREAKING DOWN

Many times we tend to procrastinate and turn our backs on responsibilities because the task(s) is too overwhelming at the time. We simply shut down like a blown fuse on an overloaded circuit.

Try the following procedure:

1. Take a break for thirty minutes or so to decrease your emotional and physical anxieties.
2. Write down the whole task at hand.
3. Break the task down in writing to as many steps as possible.
4. Develop this task list into a reasonable timeline.
5. Logically determine the amount of time each aspect will take instead of emotionally overexaggerating this time frame.
6. Implement and monitor your timeline.

## HAVE TOOLS READY

If you were trying to build a home, you might say to yourself, "This is an overwhelming and daunting task." However, if the local home improvement supplier were to drop off all the supplies and equipment you need, then you could begin to gauge how to get the chore off the ground. You might say, "Okay, I'll need to do this first with this, and next, I'll put these pieces together to create the frame," and so on.

Similarly, gathering the tools you need prior to starting an intimidating task will make it easier and much more probable you will do it.

This means:

- If you are observing a teacher, have all the information and items ready to do so before you do it.
- If you have a report due, gather all the data on your desk before you leave so it is ready and waiting the next day.

- If you are a teacher planning a new lesson, have everything you need on the desk (or in the class) before you leave the day before.

In a 2014 article by Susan Ricker in *CareerBuilder*, a company conducted a survey of a large pool of managers and workers. The objective was to find the most frequent time-wasters in the workplace and how people misappropriate their time when they are not putting their noses to the grindstone. Here are the percentages and top ten rankings of what they do instead of work[1]:

- using a cell phone or texting (50 percent)
- gossiping (42 percent)
- surfing the web (39 percent)
- catching up on social media (38 percent)
- taking a food or smoking break (27 percent)
- distractions by coworkers (24 percent)
- meetings (23 percent)
- e-mail (23 percent)
- being interrupted socially by coworkers (23 percent)
- coworkers creating distractions, like putting calls on speaker phone (10 percent)

## USE TECHNOLOGY TO YOUR ADVANTAGE

There are a host of applications for every smartphone to allow you to plan events and decrease the tendency toward procrastinating. Simply entering the word "procrastination" into an application store will bring up several apps to serve as a technology tool that will be ever present on your belt or in your purse.

## BE A "PRO"ACTIVE PROFESSIONAL

Doing as much you can on the front end of tasks as opposed to waiting until they are due can go a long way toward eliminating the stressors that wind up creating the roots for procrastination. Whenever and wherever possible, look for opportunities to complete responsibilities ahead of time as opposed to simply waiting as they come down the seemingly infinite pike of tasks.

## NOTE

1. Susan Ricker, "The 10 Biggest Productivity Killers at Work," *CareerBuilder*, 12 June 2014, http://advice.careerbuilder.com/posts/infographic-the-10-biggest-productivity-killers-at-work (accessed 12 September 2016).

## *Chapter Nine*

# Balancing Life and Home

> It's all about quality of life and finding a happy balance between work and friends and family.—Phillip Green

As an educator or administrator, time is a commodity. With so many expectations and responsibilities tugging at us in every direction, we can become stretched and extended to a point that it is hard to recognize what are the priorities and what is the horizon.

Balance can be difficult when all of the demands of work as well as home clash and leave us wondering what to do. There is no way to inoculate yourself from all of these demands completely. What you can do is make yourself more efficient and establish priorities to give yourself the best means of staying above water in the rip currents that lie ahead.

## DON'T ONLY CREATE LISTS TO BE CROSSED OFF

If you create lists at home such as vacuum, clean the house, carpool, and so forth, what you will find is that you never come to the end of your list. The list will continue to grow infinitely and you will be driven by the lists rather than utilizing the lists as tools to balance your productivity.

Allow me to explain further. Every day when you come home, you will have repeating events that must be done (making dinner, preparing yourself and your children for school the next day, etc.). Other events, however, are those that you want to get done, which can monopolize an inordinate amount of time. These are the activities that can take an entire day of the weekend and encroach seriously upon family time. So instead, set a time limit to these activities.

For example, instead of saying, "We will clean the house today" (an activity that is nonspecific in nature and can wind up taking an entire day), state, "We will clean as much as we can of the house until 12:00 and then defer the remainder until the next day." You are now managing your time instead of the schedule managing you.

## KEEP A WRITTEN ORGANIZER OF YOUR DAYS

Most of us keep some sort of written organizer, though there are some us that would rather keep it "all in our heads." The difficulty with this is that those items circulate around our heads over and over again as we juggle to remember the same three or four items that we must do.

Keeping a written organizer is common sense. Nevertheless, just writing items down is not enough. Prioritizing tasks is often helpful and prevents procrastination or confusion as to what to complete first. Labeling items with a simple "1, 2, 3" or "A, B, C" allows you to recognize what items are due or must be completed first.

Additionally, taking the list from one day and deferring those activities not finished to the next day keeps items from falling between the cracks.

## CAN'T SLEEP? TRY THIS . . .

At times, when we can't maintain the homeostasis between work and home life, it begins to seriously impact our sleep. When the world is quiet, our brains decide this is the perfect time to begin to whirl an endless stream of thoughts about home, work, and everything else like a dryer batting around a pair of sneakers.

Usually, these thoughts occur on a Sunday before the outset of the upcoming work week and leave you tired, anxious, and worried about the next day. You feel overwhelmed, utterly exhausted, and frustrated as you begin the long haul of Monday that begins a seemingly endless week ahead.

Try these activities when you are not able to sleep:

- Keep a journal by your bedside and jot down what you are thinking as it arrives in your brain. Do not worry how strange, dumb, or odd your thoughts may be; write them directly from your brain to the paper. The next day, debate these thoughts when you have a more rational frame of mind and look toward outcome-based solutions. Concurrently, glance at these each night after when you cannot sleep.
- Consider using "white noise" such as rain, a fan, calming music, or a relaxation sound application on your smartphone. This will help your mind drown out all the extraneous noise and thoughts in your head.
- Avoid television or using technology for an hour before going to bed. Technology and television keep your mind active and do not provide an opportunity for your brain to begin the natural cycle of becoming rested.
- Develop a routine, such as meditation, a calming bath, or quiet time for yourself, one hour before sleep. If you do not schedule and carve out this time each night, it will not be provided to you, so you must protect it aggressively.

## RECOGNIZE WHAT IS IMPORTANT AND PUT THINGS IN PERSPECTIVE

One thing you know for certain is that, as sure as death and taxes, public schools will always be here. You will have students and faculty; curriculums will come and go; new technologies and issues will come up each academic year. With this in mind, remember: faces change but parallel situations will always be present.

What you will never be able to get back is time spent with your family and your children growing up. Never sacrifice what you do for your own children for your students. If you have to make a choice, remember "your core"; that is your nuclear family, for they are the ones that depend on you most and are your foundation.

## YOU CAN'T BE THERE FOR EVERYBODY ALL THE TIME

If you don't learn to set limits, limits set you. Know what you are capable of and what you are not. You cannot be a member of every committee, every volunteer activity, and every carpool. Saying "no" when you need to and having a strong support network to lean on goes a long way in the work and family balance.

Remember guilt is not your friend in this case. Guilt will eat you up if you let it, and people can (and will) use it if they recognize that it will drive you to do what they want. Guilt will be there as a steering wheel to control you for those savvy enough to play on it.

Ask for the help of your spouse and family members. Oftentimes, we think "they should know what I need." Don't expect others to be mind readers. No matter how long you have known them or been together, they will still likely lack that very skill. When we are wrapped up in our own situations, we forget the others who may need us most. That does not mean, however, that the other significant members in your life don't want to help. Dividing and conquering is better than trying to do it all and failing.

Whenever possible, try to delegate and learn to accept a satisfactory completion of a task versus "well, that is not the way I would do it if I had the time." Sometimes, we must accept a "good enough" attitude and move on with more important aspects of our day.

Failure of fellow faculty to offer assistance does not necessarily mean that they don't care about you. Rather, it can mean that they did not know you needed them to focus on you or a particular issue. That is a big difference.

## TRY TO SIMPLIFY

Often we make things more complicated than they may need to be. Wherever and whenever possible, simplify. Do not try to keep up with the Joneses by having your children involved in every activity every day of the week. Like you, and the students you have taught, everyone needs some downtime.

The best way of handling issues may be the old K.I.S.S. (Keep It Simple Stupid) Method of being direct with the fewest steps necessary or possible. Not everything has to be a big issue or a complex puzzle.

## DON'T TURN TO OTHER THINGS THAT GET IN YOUR WAY

A short yet vitally important note: if you find alcohol, food, or other substances getting in the way of balancing your life—or alternatively you find these are the way to keep everything "in check"—you have a problem.

You may try to minimize, rationalize, or do any other manner of trying to grapple with this by yourself. However, if these are the things you turn to in order to "get through the day," you have an immense problem.

As it says below, get help. If you are not sure if you need support, let a professional aid you in making that decision. Clearly, your mind's lens is too fogged with your own thoughts and you need a third party to help you through this situation.

It is not weakness but strength if you realize what you need to be well and be the best parent, educator, and person you can for all that depend on you.

## GET PROFESSIONAL HELP

If anxiety or worry gets in the way of your normal functioning at school, at home, or both, don't be afraid to reach out. When emotions overtake your ability to function productively and you cannot find a means of handling it, asking for help both professionally and personally shows an amazing amount of strength. Often we are the first to offer this suggestion to others and be there as the backbone for everyone else and the last to take the advice ourselves. If you need help, get it and do so sooner rather than later. Seek counseling and/or utilize your school district's Employee Assistance Program (EAP) should they have one available. You will be glad you did.

*Chapter Ten*

# Staying Clear of Burnout

Better to burn out than rust out.—Neil Young

Many of us in helping professions such as education, social work, counseling, and medical fields do not recognize the high emotional toll that such jobs take on our psyche. It is very difficult to ask a person to put the work of caring for students in one aspect then shut your eyes and heart to what you see many of the students (and faculty) going through on a daily basis, especially when you see the emotional turmoil and struggles that many of us could hardly imagine being subjected to.

When we do not have a means of addressing these feelings in an effective manner, over the years we are worn down like stones in a rapidly moving river until we have nothing left. This, in turn, is how the concept of burnout sneaks up on us until we are just a fraction of the educator we once were. Hence is the insidious and slowly creeping nature of burnout. The book *Boundaries* by Dr. Henry Cloud and Dr. John Townsend, published in 1992, states, "Part of taking responsibility, or ownership, is knowing what is our job and what isn't. Workers who continually take on duties that aren't theirs will eventually burn out."[1] The book also offers the sage advice that if you do not establish clear boundaries, "they will be communicated indirectly or through manipulation," namely, passive-aggressive means such as "forgetting" to do what you promised, leading to further frustration and conflict.

## KNOW THE SIGNS OF BURNOUT

- A feeling of emptiness where you previously showed excitement about most facets of your job.
- Lacking energy to conduct the basic functions of your career—excessive procrastination when you did not do so previously.
- Feeling ill or excessively tired or getting sick more easily than before.
- Loss of interest in your job duties, faculty, and students.
- Excessive absences.
- You are having more "bad" than "good" days.
- Having an excessive negative attitude toward your school or job.

## HOW DO I KNOW I AM "BURNING OUT" AND NOT "STRESSING OUT"?

On the surface, being stressed may parallel a great deal of the characteristics leading to "burn out." However, the symptoms of burnout are more insidious. When you are stressed out, you tend to overreact to everything and have a lot of energy (albeit ineffective and uncomfortable energy). When you are burnt out, that energy is not present and you no longer care or can muster up the energy to do the needed obligations of your responsibilities. Whereas when you are stressed everything is an emergency in nature, when you are burnt out, nothing is important. Hence, you then demonstrate guilt for not caring about even the most important aspects of your career.

## WHAT LEADS TO BURNOUT?

Burnout can be caused by a number of factors; however, when you do not balance work and life outside of your career, it can swiftly become a pathway to burnout. Additionally, when your priorities become skewed such that work becomes the hallmark of your life at the neglect of everything else, it will eventually lead you to the precipice of burnout. Finally, if you don't appreciate the work you do as having some significance in the world or you yourself feel underappreciated, it will lead to a cycle that inevitably can lead to burnout.

## CHECK YOUR PHYSICAL AND MENTAL HEALTH FIRST

If you are burnt out or are feeling not right, first and foremost check your physical and mental health via a qualified physician or mental health professional respectively.

Some of us may say, "I simply don't have time to go to another appointment." Ask yourself this question: "Will I have the ability to withstand the long-term effects to my career or health if I don't take an hour or two out of my week?"

## HOW DO I COMBAT BURNOUT?

Burnout can sneak up and overtake you before you know it. When it has you in its grip, you may be very surprised. It can be a generally slow, gradual process that you hardly notice until you are in its grasp, and then it is too late.

So what can you do to pull yourself out of the jaws of burnout?

1. *Make time to relax:* Schedule a time each day to relax. Whether mediating, reading a book of your own interest, or taking a walk in the park, you must make time for you each and every day. You may make the case, "I simply don't have

time" or "That is selfish." No, it is not selfish. It is self-centered, and just as you nourish your body with food, you must nourish your psyche and soul with a time to disconnect from the world. After all, is it selfish to secure time to recharge your batteries so you can be the best you can for your students, faculty, family, friends, and yourself?

2. *Take up a hobby:* If you do not have some activity that you enjoy doing outside of work, then work will often spill into that empty time. If you are not balanced, your job can fill that void and lead you to an unbalanced and unfulfilling lifestyle. If you do not have any hobbies per se, look online, as there are several hobby quizzes that you can take to determine possibilities. Also, look at your personality and interests. Perhaps pick up on some interest you had as a child, or even visiting a hobby or craft store may pique your interests further.
3. *Avoid work technology when not working:* In this world of constant communication, we are never far from work or obligations if a phone is always at our hip. If you have a tendency to always check your phone or the web for the latest goings-on at school or obligations, you cannot rest. Take some time away from looking at anything work related when you are not there so that you are truly away from the chains of the job.
4. *Take care of yourself:* It goes without saying that eating and sleeping right as well as taking care of yourself physically and mentally will only serve to further insulate you from the demands of work and the scourge of burnout.
5. *Avoid negativity:* If you are around negative people, you will become a negative person. No matter how positive you are, the constant and unending negativity that you brush up against will eventually become contagious. Spend time with positive people and likely the very opposite will be true.

6. *Don't turn to things that lead to more problems:* As mentioned earlier, alcohol, overeating, illicit substances, and other addictive behaviors can take you down a vicious cycle. If you need help, get help; this cannot be overstated.

## EVALUATE YOUR JOB . . . EVALUATE YOUR LIFE

If you are to a point where you feel numb or unmotivated in your career, step away for a few hours to ask yourself why this is. It is important to dissect your feelings as to what is causing this. If you don't eventually take this step, you will continue to beat yourself up as your half-hearted attempts to get through the day will only be moderately successful.

Ask yourself:

- Why do I no longer feel satisfied in my job responsibilities? Can I pinpoint a specific time that this began?
- Is there something at home or in my life that is contributing to or causing this feeling?
- Has anything changed in my work or home life?
- Do I feel appreciated or underappreciated in my roles at work or home? If so, by whom and what would I need to change this?
- Am I physically at my best? Am I mentally at my optimal state of functioning? Who can help me get there?
- Do I have a strong network of coworkers and family support? How can I lean on them more or secure a more supportive work, social, and family network?
- Am I taking on too much? Who can I delegate responsibilities to? What responsibilities can I take off my shoulders to focus on my primary duties?

## TIME FOR A CHANGE?

If you feel you have done everything you can to address burnout and still can't seem to remedy or fix this by the abovementioned strategies, you may be considering a change. Do not take such a decision lightly. Remember, any change (good or bad) has its own stress, and as the tried and true adage goes, "the grass is not always greener on the other side."

## SOME THINGS TO CONSIDER IF YOU ARE GOING TO MAKE A CHANGE

- Decide what kind of change to make:
  - Are you wanting to change job responsibilities?
  - Change grades?
  - Change schools or districts?
  - Totally change careers?
- Am I not being recognized for my talents?
  - Have I refined my skills so that they are worthy of being recognized?
  - What would I need to know I am being recognized? Have I asked for feedback?
  - Do I advertise or market my talents?
  - Have I looked outside my school or district to "put feelers out"?
- Positives and negatives:
  - Do a checklist of the positives and negative of your potential options and see which possibility outweighs the alternatives.
- Is it just a matter of a bad school culture?

- Will that change?
- Is it within the school or the district?
- What can I do to influence the culture?

## NOTE

1. Henry Cloud and John Sims Townsend, *Boundaries: When to Say Yes, When to Say No to Take Control of Your Life* (Grand Rapids, MI: Zondervan, 1992).

*Chapter Eleven*

# Is There a Way to Do This More Productively and Effectively?

Focus on being productive instead of busy.—Tim Merris

How much of our day is wasted away at time-consuming empty meetings, at meaningless professional development, or just in idle time? Your time is ever more precious, and the way that you manifest how you use that time is ever more critical.

In this chapter, we will discuss how to take the limited amount of time and stretch it into something that is more productively and efficiently utilized. We will discuss time wasters and means of gaining time. The importance is not just making time, but how to put that time you have to a meaningful use.

## YOUR TIME IS PRECIOUS

Oftentimes we feel guilt when we try to put limits on the amount of time for others' use. We allow students, peers, and faculty to take more of our time than is warranted with empty, and unneeded, waste.

Please understand this is not to say you shouldn't listen and give what others need. What it means is recognizing when you are going down the road of an infinite cycle of nonproductive communication that leads to continued rehashing of the same topic over and over with nothing getting accomplished. It is akin to continuing to spin your wheels in the mud while not getting anywhere and just continuing to try the same strategy more diligently in hopes that the mud dries or the wheels gain traction.

If you (and the other party) are doing the same strategy, then identical results will occur, or as better stated by the proverbial genius of our time Albert Einstein, "Insanity is doing the same thing over and over again and expecting different results."

## PROVIDE A TIME FRAME FOR EVERYTHING

If you are meeting with a faculty member, parent, or student, be certain that you know your time frame for the meeting. This way you manage your day versus allowing the time to manage you.

1. When you are meeting with the other party, be certain that you both know the time frame you have to meet.
2. Try to be as proactive as possible by being prepared for the conference so you can avoid wasting time.
3. Try to determine a specific goal in your meeting.
4. As you are getting to the final minutes of a meeting, review what was discussed, which gives a tacit indication that you are concluding this meeting. Simultaneously, this allows the other person(s) to know you have heard and understand their concerns.
5. If possible, position yourself so that the clock is located behind and over the head of the person you are speaking with. This avoids you having to look at your watch or your phone for the time, which may be considered rude or indicative that you are bored with the discussion.

## PLAN AHEAD FOR THE LARGER MEETINGS

Sometimes there may be a need for an "emergency meeting" to address issues of safety or the welfare of a student in a school. The vast majority of the time, however, our meetings are planned and intentional. Yet, many times conferences can degrade to going over the same issue(s) over and over again and become stuck on a treadmill of inaction, wasting the time for all involved. This leads inevitably to increasing levels of frustration and emotion among one or all parties.

1. Before a meeting is established, you should have an agenda of what you hope to accomplish. Sounds simple enough, right? Well, how many times have you been to a meeting in which you did not know what was to be accomplished? Be certain that everyone knows the objectives.
2. Sometimes as an educator/administrator, you will get a phone call that a parent wants to come in for a meeting "and will tell you why when they get there." You have no idea why, what is needed, or even who should be involved. This sets the precedent for a very frustrating and unproductive meeting. A parent has the right to ask to meet, but they also need to be reminded that in order for you to be productive, certain ground rules need to be on the table: a basic reason for a meeting and what they hope to accomplish by meeting. Only then can you truly have an opportunity to prepare for a useful meeting.
3. We all have them: faculty who have a knack for saying the wrong thing, those who when their mouths open, you can smell the shoe leather from inserting their foot in it all too many times. When we have a meeting, we should know (for the most part) who is going to say what. We should also, more importantly, know who shouldn't say what and avoid everyone saying the same thing.

There is nothing more frustrating and disheartening in a conference than when each educator says the same thing to a family in slightly different ways because they all feel we have to participate in the conversation. This not only can waste time going down the wrong road, it can hurt a relationship that can take a long time to build between yourself and the other stakeholders.

Often meetings go smoothly, and we leave relieved that it could have been a hostile interaction. Conversely, sometimes we are "blindsided" by seemingly innocuous meetings that go terribly wrong. If possible, when having a meeting, having a general plan as to what to do should things go south is very useful. Training the faculty to be proactive in how we deal with conferences should they "go south" is always useful. Just as we plan for fire and crisis drills, we should plan for potential problematic meetings. This will also help avoid faculty making "false promises" to parents that cannot be fulfilled.

4. Meetings are not meant to go on forever. After a certain point, anything positive that is going to be gleaned from a meeting is done, and a backslide to a lack of productivity and negative communication starts to occur. Therefore, a definitive time frame for a meeting should be established. If you do not, you risk a negative interaction with a parent, and if you have others waiting to see you, you have already established a potential point of irritation for all subsequent meetings. You now will create a "domino effect" of late meetings for the rest of the day.
5. Be aware that some families, when you wish to conclude your time together, will "drop a bomb." That is, toward the end of a meeting, they will bring up an important topic to give fresh fuel to carry the meeting on to some indefinite

point. To this end, advise them that you heard this concern and will reschedule to discuss this issue at another date.

There is a very real tendency to "take the bait," so to speak, of a parent telling you some tasty morsel of information in the waning minutes of a meeting. Avoid "the bait" at all costs, as this provides the parents an opportunity to step over the boundary of a slated meeting time and thus continue the meeting at the peril of all those parents waiting and the staff held hostage from doing other necessary duties. Of course, if it is of an emergent nature, you have no choice but to address issues of safety.

Don't have a meeting just for the sake of having a meeting. Sometimes we just set up committees or have meetings simply because we don't know what to do next. That is great, provided you have a purpose and are not just using this as an empty opportunity for all parties to get together with no agenda, potential plan, or (at the very least) foundation of suggestions to get your time together off the ground.

## RISE AND SHINE EARLY

It stands to logic that if you get up earlier, you have more time to do things. If you have a family who are not early risers, you will find the quiet time can be a great period in the day to collect yourself and complete chores or other activities that would otherwise be difficult or impossible.

Some people find journaling or meditating or just reading in those quiet wee hours of the morning helps to center them for the chaos of the day ahead. The point is this is slated out as your time and cannot be monopolized by another and allows you to be as close to 100 percent as possible as you begin the day.

Likewise, if you get to school earlier (if possible), you can start with activities unfettered by the chains of obligations, clamor, and distractions that others place upon you throughout the regular school schedule.

## STAY A FEW MINUTES LATER AND CLEAR YOUR DESK

Simply organizing your desk and leaving the paperwork for the next task you have visible for the next day will help you come in motivated. It is far more inspiring to visualize coming to school the next day with a well-organized desk and the one most important item staring you in the face when you arrive, versus a pile of papers and responsibilities littering your desk and overwhelming you.

## DON'T SIGN UP FOR EVERYTHING

Some of us believe that the greater quantity of committees we join in school the better we look. Not necessarily, because quality is just as important (if not more) than quantity on how you serve your school and district.

Also, if it significantly impacts your actual job or family obligations, the trade-off may simply not be worth the time or effort. Don't fool yourself into being a martyr, that you "have" to be the one to do it or no one will. Remember, you cannot work harder than everyone else and anticipate that you can motivate them accordingly.

## WHEN YOU NEED TO DO SOMETHING IMPORTANT, TRY NOT TO BE INTERRUPTED

If you have a vital task to do, try to avoid being interrupted. As I discussed earlier, some of us have the "open-door/classroom rule." Finding a quiet place during your prep time or moving to another place in the building where you are less likely to be interrupted helps to carve out the time needed.

## GIVE ME A BREAK

If you find yourself just staring and not going anywhere with the task at hand, give yourself a break. This may be just the time you need to get your thoughts back together. Get up and walk around, but avoid using this as a time to engage in a long-winded conversation with others that will only let you procrastinate further. It is very easy to have a fifteen-minute break turn into an hour-long postponing conversation. Manage your time and don't let the time manage you.

## REMEMBER THAT ORGANIZER?

Whether you are using a technological or paper organizer, be certain that you use this method to block out time to do what you need to do. If you do not block out time in a concrete manner, the vacuum of empty space will fill that time with something else.

Also, it feels better to cross things off of a list, and you are more likely to hold yourself accountable if it is written somewhere as opposed to just ideas floating around continuously in your head.

## WHAT IS YOUR "GOOD ENOUGH"?

If you are the kind of person that needs everything "just so," you may erase what you are doing, change it over and over again, or just procrastinate doing a certain job responsibility for fear it will not be "exactly the way you want it." You join the ranks of individuals "whose standards are high beyond reach and reason, . . . straining compulsively and unremittingly toward impossible goals and who measure their own worth entirely in terms of productivity and accomplishment," according to Dr. Martin Anthony and Dr. Richard Swinson in the 1998 book *When Perfect Isn't Good Enough.*[1]

Now, I am not suggesting you strive for mere mediocrity in all your endeavors. What I am offering is that you decide "good enough" at times. What is your level of acceptable without having perfection? You can scale back from perfection and scale up from that mediocrity to gain a happy medium point. As Dr. Brené Brown states in her 2010 *New York Times* best-selling book, *The Gifts of Imperfection*, "Yes, I am sometimes afraid, but I am also brave.[2] And, yes, I am imperfect and vulnerable, but that doesn't change the truth that I am worthy of love and belonging."

## NOTES

1. Martin M. Antony and Richard P. Swinson, *When Perfect Isn't Good Enough: Strategies for Coping with Perfectionism* (Oakland, CA: New Harbinger Publications, 1998).
2. Brené C. Brown, *The Gifts of Imperfection: Let Go of Who You Think You're Supposed to Be and Embrace Who You Are* (Philadelphia: Hazelden Information & Educational Services, 2010).

*Chapter Twelve*

# Putting It All Together

> The pieces of the puzzle have a tendency to come together when you least expect it.—Jane Green

It is easy to utilize one particular skill when attempting to be likable, productive, or effective. It is like remembering to ride a bike by reminding yourself to simply pedal. Of course, there are other skills such as keeping the handlebars straight, looking ahead, and learning how to stand up on the pedals while going up hills.

If you are an educator in the modern world, putting everything together is more like pedaling a unicycle, while spinning a dish on each hand, blindfolded, in the dark, on a tightrope. Trying to do it all is a daunting if not at times impossible task.

In this final chapter, we are going to summarize what it takes to put all the pieces of the puzzle together and do so in a synergistic manner. As you can imagine, it is not just one skill that fosters success (although each helps); it is the bonding of all the attributes that allow you the very best chance at being the very best educator you can be in the areas discussed in this book.

## BALANCE KINDNESS WITH BOUNDARY SETTING

Be kind to everyone you come in contact with. You never know who you will need to assist your students or faculty, and burning bridges only leads you to be an island unto yourself with no resources.

That being said, be certain people know your values and boundaries. Be assured they understand and are clear about your values and that you're there for the safety and education of the students first and foremost. This needs to be shown early and often in your interactions with others. In these exchanges, you must be firm and assertive without coming across as overly passive and vague or too aggressive and bullying in nature.

## BE A GOOD LISTENER AND TAKE IN ALL THAT IS BEING SAID

An educator is a lifelong learner in not just the academic areas but in how to better relate with all the stakeholders and faculty that we come across on a regular basis. This means being an open and a good listener.

Each and every person you come in contact with has a story and is capable of teaching you something. Don't just hear but truly listen to what is being said—and also not being said. Question, clarify, and ask follow-up inquiries to be certain you know what is intended before responding.

Listen to what you want to hear as well as what you don't want to hear, and remember that some of the best information you can glean is from the criticism of others. Say what you mean and mean what you say and encourage others to do the very same.

Avoid the trap of using alternative means of communication (such as the Internet) that serve to mask much of what is said, as it hides the nonverbal cues so vital in all dialogue.

## KNOW YOUR PRIORITIES AND YOUR VALUES

If you do not know what is important as well as the order of such things, you will ultimately lose sight of these values and not know which way is up.

Develop a strong statement, a statement of your value, vocational purpose, and priorities, and make certain that your comprehension of this is second nature to you. When any issue comes up, be certain that it falls into your list of priorities and values system before you engage in it accordingly.

Remember as well that you must keep "your core" beliefs and your health and needs paramount or you will be of little or no use to those who depend on you at home as well as at school.

Be aware that your personal mental and physical health are paramount. You are only as happy and effective as those two areas of your lifestyle permit you to be. This means not sacrificing these elements of your life for any other portion of your job or other external obligations. Again, it means setting limits and not using these boundaries to fuel your own guilt. As the old adage goes, "work to live" versus "live to work."

Finally, be aware of those inside as well outside of school that can test or try your values. Avoid those that gossip, offer you false praise or drama, or attempt to bully or "backslap" you out of your values or priorities on a regular basis.

## RECOGNIZE THE CULTURAL BACKDROP IN EVERYTHING AND ANYTHING YOU DO

When you are communicating with others, you have a tendency to think how and why you think a certain way is correct (a.k.a. the "Attribution Bias"). So often, things that are vitally important are pushed to the side in honor of your belief system. Cultural dynamics are a critical and key aspect of the environmental factors that will test your belief system and knowledge.

Unfortunately, we don't know what we don't know about cultures, so we have a tendency to walk into situations that can be deemed offensive without even knowing it. Further, generationally, there are cultural values that shift from age group to age group. Therefore, it is vital to try to understand the backdrop of culture as a means of best relating to, and not offending, others.

## LISTENING: A RARE SKILL INDEED

Spending time listening is invariably more useful than spending time talking. Yet, it is a very rare skill that is often pushed to the back burner by the fallacy that always being extroverted and talking incessantly is better than taking a step back and soaking in what is being said and telegraphed.

To further confuse this effort is that in active and productive communication, more and more people are turning to texting, e-mail, and other forms of technological speaking that don't require the skill of listening. Nor do they provide practice on the task of the hard work of understanding and comprehending fully what your fellow human beings are saying around you.

According to a 1957 article written by Ralph G. Nichols and Leonard A. Stevens in *The Harvard Business Review*, "Two months after listening to a talk (i.e., training), the average listener will remember only about 25% of what was said."[1] This testing was conducted in multiple universities with the same results. In other words, your ability to listen and retain more than 25 percent of the information stated will put you at a decidedly distinct advantage over others.

## GETTING STARTED

As more and more tasks and responsibilities are anticipated from educators on all levels, the habit of procrastinating becomes more engrained.

It is important to know the means of recognizing and addressing procrastination. Not allowing perfectionism or fear of bigger tasks that become overwhelming to stand in your way is a vital skill. Avoidance of pushing things to the last minute and then beating yourself up for their not being completed to your level of satisfaction is necessary for your very survival.

Further, balancing home and school life is a delicate homeostatic juggle. If you lean too much on one side, there are serious consequences that ultimately affect every other aspect of your life. Therefore, it is important to develop a means to balance and create a structural framework to compartmentalize both that works for your lifestyle. If you cannot find a way of getting this balance, consider outside resources and assistance to better help you in finding an equilibrium for these two most important elements of your life.

## DON'T LET BURNOUT BURN YOU

When you have exhausted all your enthusiasm and you have nothing left, you are not of any use to yourself or anyone else. Worse yet, you have a self-fulfilling prophecy of failure and then beat yourself up for your lack of motivating yourself with the spark needed to succeed.

Recognize when you are burning out. Know the signs of burnout and do something early before the habits become instilled into your daily work life. Identify that there is a difference between being stressed out and burnt out and know that one can lead to the other if not cared for.

## DON'T UNDERESTIMATE THE IMPORTANCE OF YOUR TIME

Time is the one and only commodity that you have when it comes to productivity and efficiency. If you do not manage that time, it will overtake and overwhelm you. Make certain that you recognize not only the precious nature of everyone else's time but the vitality of yours too. Just like any other profession, your time and expertise need to recognized and coveted when they are provided.

This means being able to say "no" without guilt and learning how to manage the time in other activities such as committees and meetings. Education and life are about results, not just an infinite set of meetings and dialogue.

## NOTE

1. Ralph G. Nichols and Leonard A. Stevens, "Listening to People," *Harvard Business Review*, September 1957, https://hbr.org/1957/09/listening-to-people (accessed 28 August 2016).

# Conclusion

## CONCLUSION

> Where there is a will, there is a way. If there is a chance in a million that you can do something, anything, to keep what you want from ending, do it. Pry the door open or, if need be, wedge your foot in that door and keep it open.—Pauline Kael

As an educator, in whatever role you play, you have the most important job in the world. You are the one shaping the next generation of learners and thinkers, and you are preparing each of your pupils for jobs that we may only have a vague grasp of based on our current knowledge.

As we teach students academic skills and create a climate for which to incubate those needed attributes, more and more educators of every sort are called upon to play the role of social worker, parent, administrator, and teacher all simultaneously. This means that we are no longer restricted to only teaching academic subjects.

Rather, we are now teaching through example how to relate to others and communicate in the real world. Your likability, productiveness, and efficiency cannot help but rub off on all levels of the school system as they "trickle out, down, and up" among all those that come in contact with your school.

In many ways, the social and study skills that you emulate and demonstrate will ultimately filter down to the students as well. Those habits, in turn, may do much to help them in their lives and careers ahead. After all, how many students and people do we know that are brilliant academically but cannot succeed due to the shackles of an inability to socialize or organize their work and societal lives?

As the pendulum swings back and forth and expectations change in what is expected in the school systems, some things will not. The ability to develop relationships and maintain them and the need for constant self-starting, production, and efficacy are all skills that will carry on as needed for this generation (and subsequent generations) of prospective pupils. Henceforth, it is my hope that you have learned some additional skills in these areas from this book that will carry you even further in your career and competence.

I thank you so very much for taking this time with me. As educators we are our greatest resource for inspiration and professional development. In each other, we can draw the knowledge necessary to be lifelong learners and educators.

# Appendix

FIGURE A.1

## Values

Look at each of the values below. Circle the ones that are most important to you and then prioritize the top five most vital in order from one (most important) to five (least important):

| | | | |
|---|---|---|---|
| Honesty | Fairness | Charisma | Kindness |
| Love | Optimism | Popularity | Trustworthiness |
| Honesty | Balance | Authenticity | Competency |
| Community | Caring | Loyalty | Respect |
| Beauty | Contribution | Assertiveness | Confidence |
| Leadership | Education | Perfection | Relaxation |
| Speed | Ability | Diversity | Certainty |
| Bravery | Comfort | Charity | Extroversion |
| Obedience | Modesty | Mindfulness | Intelligence |
| Charity | Family | Competence | Trust |
| Friendship | Citizenship | Faith | Fun |

| | | | |
|---|---|---|---|
| Happiness | Creativity | Growth | Security |
| Wealth | Status | Fairness | Ability |
| Diligence | Empathy | Fitness | Humor |
| Vision | Teamwork | Service | Professionalism |
| Expertise | Drive | Achievement | Acknowledgement |
| Introversion | Heart | Compassion | Neatness |
| Hygiene | Guidance | Freedom | Energy |

The above list and your priorities help to best detail what are the qualities and values you find most important. Further, they will allow you to provide a grasp of these merits when interacting with others in all facets of your position.

Write Down Your Top Five (In Order First to Fifth) Below:

1. ___________________
2. ___________________
3. ___________________
4. ___________________
5. ___________________

FIGURE A.2

## Questions

1. I like to give someone a pat on the back once in a while; that is just the way I do things. There is nothing wrong with that, right? True/False
2. All of us have embraced the technology revolution. Everyone is aware of how to basically operate a smartphone, is on social media, and is proficient on the Internet. It is a survival skill. True/False

3. There are about fifty recognized holidays among all religions and I am aware of most of them. True/False
4. In the United States, all people strive for equality and fairness and try their very best "to get ahead" within a natural system of competition and capitalism. True/False
5. In various regions of the United States, different people have different cultural perspectives based on the places that they live. True/False
6. It is better to be outgoing and extroverted then ingoing and introverted culturally. True/False
7. Some cultures are more formal and others less formal in how they relate to others. True/False
8. In certain cultures, it is considered rude to go right to discussing important topics without first engaging in small talk. True/False
9. Due to your job as an educator, some people may not directly address concerns with you and may tend to be less obvious about worries. True/False
10. Each school system and school has its own unique culture. True/False

## Answers

1. False. Cultures such as Orthodox Judaism and Islam do not allow contact between males and females of any type unless they are married. It is considered taboo to be alone in a room with a member of the opposite sex who is not your spouse and should be avoided so as to not even display a hint of impropriety.
2. False. Technology is not embraced as quickly (or at all) by certain generations. The Baby Boomers (in general) are more skeptical and less likely to utilize technology the way the subsequent generations do. Forcing technology upon those

who fear it without adequate training may lead to a backlash or a refusal to use it in academics.

3. False. There are more than one hundred holidays recognized by the New Jersey Department of Education and many you or other faculty may not be aware of fully. Also, the way in which certain persons celebrate a religion may vary greatly. Therefore, what some groups find as a "less important" holiday, others may find as more critical to recognize and do so accordingly.
4. False. Some cultures are based on an age-old system of hierarchy. They base their system on familial history and may consider it inappropriate to attempt to compete with others as they consider the whole of the group over the needs of the individual. Additionally, there may be some cultural clashes as the old-world ways of addressing this are met with modern methods from generation to generation.
5. True. In the United States, people tend to have various political, cultural, and economic views that vary from region to region. This includes politics, views on "hot button" issues, and cultural makeup as a whole.
6. False. Although in our culture extroversion and being friendly is looked upon positively, it is not the case in all cultures. Many Eastern cultures have a far greater emphasis on those people that are introverted and seek wisdom versus outwardly leaning personality types.
7. True. Many cultures have age-old formal practices centered on family, religion, and dining from which members rarely deviate. In general, the American culture is looked at as being less formal and traditional as a whole.
8. True. In the Italian American culture, it is generally considered "rude" to jump right into a discussion of business matters without first engaging in small talk to get to know and comfort the other individual. This is true in several other

cultures as well. In contrast, other cultural dynamics get "right to business" and the heart of the matter and believe small talk to be a deceitful means of "kissing up" to the other party.

9. True. In Eastern and other cultures, educators are held in the highest esteem. In many countries, teachers are ranked near or at the top in terms of respect and admiration. This means that questioning an educator may seem as though you are questioning their competence or integrity. Doing so is forbidden and so they will not challenge you or respond in a critical fashion to your statements.
10. True. We have all heard of the notion of school climate, and it is certainly true that due to the socioeconomic, regional, and faculty makeup of each school, they all have idiosyncratic cultures that are very different from each other.

    This means that if you truly want to know a school, you must avoid merely sitting in your classroom or your office. Instead, you must try to be "a fly on the wall" and just absorb what you see and hear as you go through the halls, classrooms, faculty rooms, and sporting events. In doing so, you can tell a lot of what is going on and comprehend the proverbial culture climate and temperature within the school or district that you are serving.

# Bibliography

Antony, Martin M., and Richard P. Swinson. *When Perfect Isn't Good Enough: Strategies for Coping with Perfectionism.* Oakland, CA: New Harbinger Publications, 1998.

Baldoni, John. "Managing Big Egos So the Entire Team Wins." *Harvard Business Review.* 19 February 2009. https://hbr.org/2009/02/managing-big-egos-so-the-entir (accessed 10 October 2016).

Brown, Brené C. *The Gifts of Imperfection: Let Go of Who You Think You're Supposed to Be and Embrace Who You Are.* Philadelphia: Hazelden Information & Educational Services, 2010.

Cain, Susan. *Quiet: The Power of Introverts in a World That Can't Stop Talking.* New York: Crown Publishers, 2002.

Carnegie, Dale, Dorothy Carnegie, and Arthur R. Pell. *How to Win Friends and Influence People.* New York: Simon & Schuster, 1936.

Cloud, Henry, and John Sims Townsend. *Boundaries: When to Say Yes, When to Say No to Take Control of Your Life.* Grand Rapids, MI: Zondervan, 1992.

Cohen, Jennifer. "How Likeable Are You? Here Are 8 Ways You Can Improve Your Likeability at Work." *Forbes.* 7 April 2014. http://www.forbes.com/sites/jennifercohen/2014/04/07/how-likeable-are-you-here-are-8-ways-you-can-improve-your-likeability-at-work/#6dfa2a9f1596.

Cone, Mariah. "Churn: The High Cost of Principal Turnover." Academia.edu—Share Research (accessed 29 October 2016).

Cridlan, Caryn. "Attribution Biases—How Do You See the World?" Mediate.com. http://www.mediate.com/articles/CridlandC3.cfm (accessed 8 October 2016).

Fonseca, Todd A. "The 4 Steps to Mirroring Successfully." *Science of People.* August 2015. http://www.scienceofpeople.com/2015/08/the-power-of-mirroring/ (accessed 30 October 2016).

Formica, Michael J. "How To Stay in the Present Moment—Don't Chop Water When You Should Be Carrying Wood." *Peace and Freedom*. 31 January 2014. https://johnib.wordpress.com/tag/dont-chop-water-when-you-should-be-carrying-wood (accessed 15 September 2016).

Frindte, Wolfgang, and Daniel Geschke. "Stanley Milgram: Obedience to Authority. An Experiment View. Harper & Row: New York 1974, 224 S. (dt. Das Milgram-Experiment. Zur Gehorsamsbereitschaft Gegenüber Autoritäten. Rowohlt Verlag: Reinbek Bei Hamburg 1974, 256 S.)." *Klassiker Der Sozialwissenschaften* (2016): 296–301.

Hammill, Greg. "Mixing and Managing Four Generations of Employees." *Fairleigh Dickinson University Magazine*, Winter/Spring 2005. http://www.fdu.edu/newspubs/magazine/05ws/generations.htm (accessed 28 August 2016).

Institute of People Management. "Building an Employee-focused Workplace Part 1—IPM." 9 May 2016. http://www.ipm.co.za/building-an-employee-focused-workplace-part-1/ (accessed 12 June 2016).

Kofman, Fred. *Conscious Business: How to Build Value through Values*. Boulder, CO: Sounds True, 2006.

Mosely, Eric. "4 Reasons Employee Appreciation Matters Year-Round." *Huffington Post*. 3 March 2016. http://www.huffingtonpost.com/eric-mosley/4-reasons-employee-apprec_b_9368584.html.

New Jersey Department of Education. "List of Religious Holidays Permitting Pupil Absence from School." http://www.state.nj.us/educaton/genfo/holiday.htm (accessed 29 September 2006).

Nichols, Ralph G., and Leonard A. Stevens. "Listening to People." *Harvard Business Review*, September 1957. https://hbr.org/1957/09/listening-to-people (accessed 28 August 2016).

Novick, Brett J. *Parents and Teachers Working Together*. Lanham, MD: Rowman & Littlefield, 2016.

Phillips, Donald T. *Martin Luther King Jr. Lessons on Leadership: Inspiration and Wisdom for Challenging Times*. New York: Warner Books, 1999.

Ricker, Susan. "The 10 Biggest Productivity Killers at Work." *CareerBuilder*. 12 June 2014. http://advice.careerbuilder.com/posts/infographic-the-10-biggest-productivity-killers-at-work (accessed 12 September 2016).

Rozenholtz, S. J. "Workplace Conditions That Affect Teacher's Quality and Commitment for Teacher Induction." *Elementary School Journal* 4 (1989): 421–38.

School Leaders Network. *Churn: The High Cost of Principal Turnover*. 2014. https://connectleadsucceed.org/sites/default/files/principal_turnover_cost.pdf.

Strutner, Suzy. "8 Cultural Differences Between America and Other Countries." *Huffington Post*. 14 September 2013. http://www.huffingtonpost.com/2013/09/14/weird-cultural-differences_n_3875360.html (accessed 28 October 2016).

Superville, Denisa R. "Principal Turnover Takes Costly Toll on Students and Districts, Report Says." *Education Week*. 7 November 2014.

"Vanessa Van Edwards." http://www.curious.com/scienceofpeople (accessed 1 November 2016).

"Villard, Henry, 1835–1900. Henry Villard Papers, 1604–1948: Guide." Harvard University Library. Last updated 11 October 1016. http://oasis.lib.harvard.edu/oasis/deliver/~hou00295 (accessed 19 October 2016).

Woodard, Colin. *American Nations: A History of the Eleven Rival Regional Cultures of North America*. New York: Viking, 2011.

# Index

# About the Author

**Brett J. Novick** holds a bachelor's degree in psychology from LaSalle University in Philadelphia and a master's degree in family therapy from Friends University in Wichita, Kansas, as well as postdegree work and certification in school social work from Monmouth University in West Long Branch, New Jersey, and education leadership from the NJEXCEL Program in Monroe, New Jersey. Mr. Novick is licensed as a marriage and family therapist and state certified as a school social worker. He holds postgraduate certification as a supervisor, principal, and school administrator.

Mr. Novick has been working within school districts in New Jersey for the past sixteen years. In addition to his work as a school social worker/counselor, he has worked in private practice as well as a variety of community mental health settings with individuals, groups, and families. He also has experience working with children and families in crisis as an in-home therapist. Mr. Novick supervised a therapeutic children's shelter for youth in the care and custody of the state of Missouri as well and was employed as a coordinator of a county program in that state for families that had a member with a developmental disability. He currently is an adjunct instructor at Rutgers University teaching postgraduate work in the subjects of dealing with difficult parents, classroom management, behavioral issues with students, practical social skills for classified students, personality disorders, special education issues, and parental enrichment.

This is Mr. Novick's second book, the first being *Parents and Teachers Working Together: Addressing School's Most Vital Stakeholders*. Additionally, he has authored several national and international articles on education, educational administration, counseling, and social work. Mr. Novick was awarded District Teacher of the Year in 2007–2008 and New Jersey School Counselors Association Human Rights Advocate of the Year in 2008. In 2011, he was honored with the New Jersey Council on Developmental Disabilities Inclusive Educator of the Year Award and Fellowship. He has received the OCPGA Ocean County Counselor of the Year Award, the Ocean County Human Services Advocate Award, the NJDOE Holocaust Education Commission's Hela Young Memorial Award, as well as the NJEA Dr. Martin Luther King Jr. Civil Award, U.S. Congressional Outstanding Achievement Award, human rights awards, and NJ DOE Exemplary Educator of the Year Awards.